ACKNOWLEDGMENTS

The author and publisher would like to thank the following individuals who reviewed the **Read On** program at various stages of development and whose comments, reviews, and assistance were instrumental in helping us shape the project:

Tony Albert
Jewish Vocational Services
San Francisco, CA

Victoria Badalamenti
LaGuardia Community College
Long Island City, NY

Lynne Telson Barsky
Suffolk Community College
Jericho, NY

Leslie Biaggi
Pembroke Pines, FL

Greg Cossu
Kyoto, Japan

Nicholas J. Dimmitt
Center for Language &
Educational Technology
Asian Institute of Technology
Pathumthani, Thailand

Edna Diolata
ELESAIR Adult ESL Program
New York, NY

Deborah Horowitz
Queens College
Flushing, NY

Bea Jensen
ELESAIR Adult ESL Program
New York, NY

Tay Lesley
Culver City Adult School
Culver City, CA

Susannah O. MacKay
Atlanta, GA

Claude Mathis
El Paso Community College
El Paso, TX

Linda O'Roke
City College of San Francisco
San Francisco, CA

Jenny Outlaw
Richmond Community College
Hamlet, NC

Mary Pierce
Xavier Adult Education Center
New York, NY

Anita Podrid
Queens College
Flushing, NY

Linda Reichman
City College of San Francisco
San Francisco, CA

Jane Selden
LaGuardia Community College
Long Island City, NY

David Thormann
City College of San Francisco
San Francisco, CA

Marjorie Vai
The New School for Social Research
New York, NY

Itsuki Yasuyoshi
Waseda University
Tokyo, Japan

    I was very fortunate to receive helpful suggestions, encouragement, and advice from many people. I am especially grateful to Erik Gundersen, Acquisitions Editor, for his clear vision on this project. He is not only my editor, but also my friend. I am sincerely indebted to Mari Vargo, the developmental editor on this project. She made herself available to me around the clock, including weekends, holidays, and whenever else I needed her, and was always right on target with the endless edits involved. I am thankful to my friends at the English Language Institute at Queens College who continue to show interest and support. Last but not least, I am ever grateful to my family for allowing me the time I needed to complete this book and for helping me keep things in perspective.

–Nancy Nici Mare

TABLE OF CONTENTS

Acknowledgments iii
Welcome to **Read On 2** vi
To the Teacher ix

CHAPTER 1   **A New Kind of Café** 2
You can play with dogs at these popular Korean cafés.

CHAPTER 2   **Day Care for Dogs** 6
Dogs don't have to stay home alone anymore!

Activity Menu • Chapters 1 and 2 10

CHAPTER 3   **Double the Fun** 12
People see double at Twins Restaurant in New York City.

CHAPTER 4   **The Underwater Hotel** 16
This hotel is 21 feet below the ocean!

Activity Menu • Chapters 3 and 4 20

CHAPTER 5   **Circus Family** 22
This father is a clown, and his family lives at the circus with him.

CHAPTER 6   **The Thrill of It** 26
This man built a roller coaster in his own backyard.

Activity Menu • Chapters 5 and 6 30

CHAPTER 7   **A Race to Get Married** 32
Two runners met at a race and got married at a race, too.

CHAPTER 8   **Married with Two Homes** 36
This happy family lives in two different cities.

Activity Menu • Chapters 7 and 8 40

CHAPTER 9   **Dream On** 42
You can learn to solve your problems while you sleep.

CHAPTER 10   **Remember to Sleep** 46
How important is sleep for your memory?

Activity Menu • Chapters 9 and 10 50

Read On 2

Nancy Nici Mare

**McGraw-Hill
Contemporary**

For Joseph, Elizabeth, and Steven.

The publisher would like to thank the following for their permission to reproduce photographs:
Cover Photo Credits: © CORBIS, © Ed Bock/CORBIS, © AP Wide World Photo, © Jason Schmidt
Interior Photo Credits: p. 2 © VAUTHEY PIERRE/CORBIS SYGMA, p. 6 © CORBIS, p. 12 © Twins Talent, p. 16 © CORBIS, p. 22 © Roger Halls; Cordaiy Photo Library Ltd./CORBIS, p. 26 © AP Wide World Photo, p. 32 © Ed Bock/CORBIS, p. 36 © Tom & Dee Ann McCarthy/CORBIS, p. 42 © CORBIS, p. 46 © Dex Images/CORBIS, p. 52 © Charles Gupton/CORBIS, p. 56 © John Henley/CORBIS, p. 62 © Darren Carroll, p. 66 © Phil Schermeister/CORBIS, p. 72 © Jason Schmidt, p. 76 © Kennan Ward/CORBIS, p. 82 © Ms. Foundation for Women, p. 86 © Jon Feingersh/CORBIS, p. 92 © ATC Productions/CORBIS, p. 96 © Tom Stewart/CORBIS

Read On 2, First Edition

This book is printed on recycled, acid-free paper containing 10% postconsumer waste.

2 3 4 5 6 7 8 9 0 QPD/QPD 0 9 8 7 6

ISBN-13: 978-0-07-282307-3
ISBN-10: 0-07-282307-0

Editorial director: Tina B. Carver
Senior managing editor: Erik Gundersen
Developmental editor: Mari Vargo
Director of North American marketing: Thomas P. Dare
Director of international marketing and sales: Kate Oakes
Production manager: Genevieve Kelley

Cover designer: Mary Jane Broadbent
Interior designer: Don Kye, Think Design LLC
Copyeditor: Sophia Wisener
Skills indexer: Talbot Hamlin
Photo researcher: Kristin Thalheimer

INTERNATIONAL EDITION ISBN: 0-07-121882-3

McGraw-Hill
Contemporary

www.mhcontemporary.com

CHAPTER 11   **A Healthy Choice** **52**
Students at this high school are learning to eat right.

CHAPTER 12   **Fun, Fit, and Free** **56**
A mayor decided to help his city lose weight and get healthy.

Activity Menu • Chapters 11 and 12 . . . . **60**

CHAPTER 13   **Senior Athletes** **62**
These busy senior citizens have their own Senior Olympics.

CHAPTER 14   **A New Life** **66**
This woman is always ready to try something new and exciting.

Activity Menu • Chapters 13 and 14 . . . . **70**

CHAPTER 15   **Elephant Art** **72**
Artists teach elephants in Southeast Asia how to paint pictures.

CHAPTER 16   **Monkey Town** **76**
At this South African zoo, only the people are in cages.

Activity Menu • Chapters 15 and 16 . . . . **80**

CHAPTER 17   **Take Our Daughters and Sons to Work Day** **82**
Children go to work with parents or other family members!

CHAPTER 18   **Teamwork** **86**
Some companies have fun ways to teach people to work together.

Activity Menu • Chapters 17 and 18 . . . . **90**

CHAPTER 19   **The Chip Family** **92**
The Jacobs are the first family to have computer chips in their arms.

CHAPTER 20   **The Right Time** **96**
Doctors say we have to "listen" to clocks inside our bodies.

Activity Menu • Chapters 19 and 20 . . . . **100**

Skills Index **102**
Vocabulary Index **103**

WELCOME TO READ ON 2

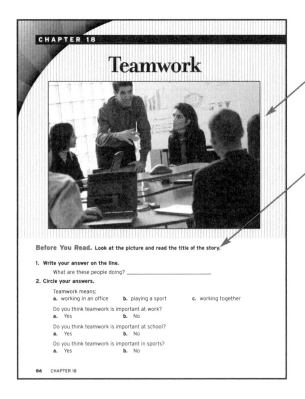

Chapter-opening photographs introduce students to the themes of the readings.

Before You Read activities ask students to make inferences, activate their prior knowledge, and answer questions based on their own experience.

Comprehension will increase for many students as they listen to **audio recordings** (available on cassette and CD) of the reading selections.

Selected **key vocabulary items** appear in bold-faced type in the readings.

Main Idea questions check students' understanding of what the reading selections are about.

By working with **standardized testing formats,** students prepare for success on a variety of standardized exams.

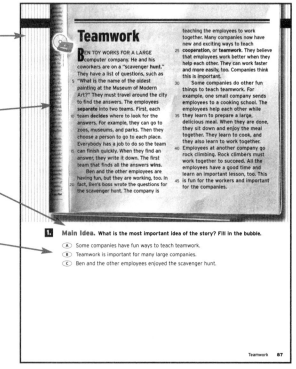

A variety of reading comprehension activities checks students' understanding of the reading passages while providing additional vocabulary practice.

Learn New Words and **Complete the Paragraph** activities test students' understanding of new vocabulary items.

2. **Just the Facts.** Check (✓) **True** or **False**. If a sentence is false, change it to make it true.

	True	False
1. Ben Toy is the boss of a large computer company. Ben Toy works for a large computer company.	☐	☑
2. The employees learn to work together on the scavenger hunt.	☐	☐
3. Ben's boss plans where to look for the answers.	☐	☐
4. Companies teach teamwork in different ways.	☐	☐
5. Some employees go to cooking schools to learn teamwork.	☐	☐
6. It's important for rock climbers to work alone.	☐	☐

3. **Learn New Words.** Choose the correct words. Write them on the lines.

choose   cooperation   decides   ~~hunt~~   separate   wins

a. The company told Ben Toy and his coworkers to go on a scavenger ___hunt___.
b. First, the employees _____ into two teams.
c. A large computer company decided to teach _____, or teamwork, to its employees.
d. Then the teams _____ a person to go to each place.
e. The first team that finds all the answers _____.
f. Each team _____ where to look for the answers.

4. **What Happened First?** With a partner, put the sentences in Activity 3 in the correct order.

a. _____ b. _____ c. __1__ d. _____ e. _____ f. _____

5. **Think It Over.** Teamwork is important for scavenger hunts, cooking, and rock climbing. What other activities are easier to do with teamwork? With a partner, write six more activities in the chart below. Share your answers.

ACTIVITIES FOR TEAMWORK	
scavenger hunts	
cooking	

In **Think It Over** activities, students use critical thinking skills to examine ideas introduced in the reading selections.

6. **Talk It Over.** Separate into two teams. With your team, write a list of ten questions about your school or your class. For example, "Who speaks three languages?" or "How many computers are in the computer lab?" Then trade lists and go on a scavenger hunt.

SCAVENGER HUNT QUESTIONS	
1.	6.
2.	7.
3.	8.
4.	9.
5.	10.

Talk It Over activities ask students to discuss ideas related to the chapter topics.

Write It Down activities ask students to write sentences and paragraphs about their thoughts, opinions, and ideas.

7. **Write It Down.** Look at the list in Activity 5. Which activity needs teamwork most? Why?

Teamwork is most important for _____ because _____

WELCOME TO READ ON 2

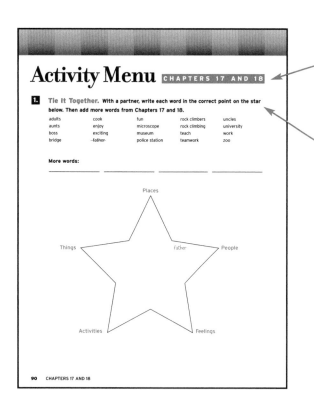

Each pair of chapters is connected by a similar theme. The **Activity Menu** ties the two chapters together, giving students opportunities to practice new vocabulary and do expansion work.

Tie It Together activities use graphic organizers to help students synthesize information from the previous two chapters.

Just for Fun activities reinforce vocabulary and give students opportunities to practice spelling and word order.

Go Online activities allow students to perform basic Internet searches.

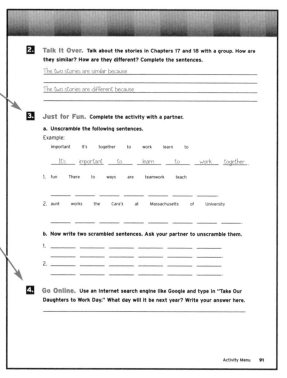

TO THE TEACHER

Read On 2 is the second in a series of two readers for beginning and high beginning students of English as a second or foreign language. **Read On 1** targets the needs of beginning students.

Each book in the **Read On** series contains 20 four-page chapters featuring short, stimulating, and accessible reading passages on high-interest topics such as a hotel that's 21 feet below the ocean and a man who built a roller coaster in his backyard. In addition, each reading contains vital, high-frequency vocabulary that is recycled throughout the chapters in the book. This gives students a chance to see new vocabulary a number of times and in a variety of contexts.

The chapters in **Read On** are self-standing and may be used in any order. Thus, the teacher has the option of either working systematically through the book, or selecting chapters according to the needs and interests of the class.

The inclusion of a two-page Activity Menu after each pair of chapters is a unique and dynamic feature of the **Read On** series. Each Activity Menu ties together content and learning objectives from the readings in the two previous chapters, giving students additional opportunities to recycle vocabulary and do expansion work. Graphic organizers help students synthesize information from each pair of chapters and Go Online activities allow students to practice Internet search skills.

Components

The complete **Read On 2** program includes the following components:

- Student Book
- Teacher's Manual with answer key, chapter quizzes, and vocabulary cloze activities for each chapter
- Audiocassette/audio CD with recordings of all reading passages

CHAPTER 1

A New Kind of Café

Before You Read. Look at the picture and read the title of the story.

1. Write your responses on the lines.

   This is a _____.

   People go there to _____.

   Do you ever go to places like this? _____.

2. Answer the questions about A New Kind of Café. Check (✓) your answers on the left.

   After you read the story, answer the questions again on the right.

| BEFORE YOU READ: | | | A NEW KIND OF CAFÉ | AFTER YOU READ: | | |
YES	NO	MAYBE	QUESTIONS	YES	NO	MAYBE
			Can you drink coffee there?			
			Can you play with dogs there?			
			Can you eat food there?			
			Can you take your dog there?			

A New Kind of Café

IN CITIES ALL OVER THE WORLD, people go to cafés to relax alone or with friends. They drink coffee and sometimes have a snack. But in many
5 cafés in Korea, you can do more than that. You can relax and play with dogs at new "dog cafés."

At the DOG Café, you can **choose** a dog to play with. The dogs are in **cages**
10 around the room. First, you choose a dog. Then it comes out of its cage. Sometimes, it sits on your lap. You can buy food for the pet, too.

The Bau House is different from the
15 DOG Café. You don't have to choose a dog at the Bau House. All the dogs sit, play, or run around, **while** people drink coffee and eat sandwiches. You can play with all the dogs at the Bau House.

20 Lori Cheong goes to the DOG Café about once a week. All the dogs there are very friendly. But Lori likes to play with Princess, her **favorite** dog. She often buys food for Princess, too. Lori
25 likes to go to the DOG Café for many reasons. "I love dogs, but I live in a small apartment in Seoul. It is **too** small for a dog. Also, dogs don't like to be alone, and I work all day." So when Lori
30 needs to have some fun with a pet, she goes to the dog café to see Princess.

Dog cafés are very **popular** in Korea, but they are not cheap. A cup of coffee costs about 4500 won (U.S.
35 $3.50). But the fun is free!

1. Main Idea. What is the most important idea of the story? Fill in the bubble.

- (A) A cup of coffee is expensive at a dog café.
- (B) Lori loves dogs, but her apartment is very small.
- (C) You can play with dogs at some cafés in Korea.

2. Just the Facts. Check (✓) True or False.

	True	False
1. People take their dogs to dog cafés in Korea.	☐	✔
2. Lori lives in a small apartment.	☐	☐
3. Lori works all day.	☐	☐
4. Lori has a dog.	☐	☐
5. Coffee is not expensive at a dog café.	☐	☐

3. Learn New Words. Circle the correct words. Write them on the lines.

1. The dogs run around together _____*while*_____ people drink and eat.

because (while) after

2. The dogs are in _____ around the room.

laps   cafés   cages

3. First, you _____ a dog. Then it comes out of its cage.

buy   play with   choose

4. Lori lives in a small apartment. It is _____ small for a dog.

too   not   usually

5. She likes to play with Princess, her _____ dog.

expensive   popular   favorite

6. Dog cafés are very _____ in Korea. Many people like to go there.

friendly   popular   expensive

4. Correct the Sentences. The underlined parts of these sentences are wrong. With a partner, rewrite the sentences with the correct information.

1. In cities all over the world, people go to cafés to play with dogs.

In cities all over the world, people go to cafés to drink coffee.

2. Lori Cheong goes to DOG Café every day.

_____

3. When Lori wants to do some work, she goes to a dog café.

_____

4. Sometimes people buy food for other people at dog cafés.

_____

5. Think It Over. **With a partner, choose three sentences to complete the chart below. Then add your own sentence to the chart.**

They sell snacks for people.

~~They sell food for dogs.~~

People can choose a dog to play with.

They sell coffee and sandwiches.

Dogs run around and play together.

They are very popular.

WHY ARE DOG CAFÉS UNUSUAL?
1. They sell food for dogs.
2.
3.
My sentence:

6. Talk It Over. **How is the Bau House different from the DOG Café? Write your answers on the lines. Then share your answers with your classmates.**

At the Bau House, _____

At the DOG Café, _____

7. Write It Down. **Do you want to go to a dog café? Why or why not? Complete the sentence and share it with your classmates.**

I (want/don't want) to go to a dog café because _____

_____

_____

_____

CHAPTER 2

Day Care for Dogs

Before You Read. Look at the picture and read the title of the story.

1. Circle your answers.

Do dogs like to be at home alone?	Yes	No
Do you have a dog?	Yes	No

How do dogs feel when they are at home alone all day?

a. They are tired. **b.** They are happy. **c.** They are lonely.

2. Write your answers on the lines.

What is this dog doing? It is _____.

Who usually goes to day care centers? _____.

Day Care for Dogs

EVERY MORNING DENISE PEREZ **takes** a walk with Jesse. After their walk, Denise **gets ready** for work. But before she goes to work,
5 she **drives** Jesse to a nearby day care center. Jesse stays there all day while Denise is at work. Jesse has lunch at the day care center. He enjoys play time and takes a nap there, too. This
10 may not seem unusual. Many people take their children to day care centers. But Jesse is not a child. He is a dog. Jesse's day care center is a place for pets.
15 Day care for dogs is very popular today. Many large cities have animal day care centers. Some pet owners, like Denise, are very happy with these day care centers. "I go to work early
20 in the morning and come home late at night. I don't like to leave Jesse at home alone all day. He gets very lonely because he has no one to play with," says Denise. "But when he
25 goes to the day care center, he can play with other dogs. He runs around and gets a lot of **exercise**. And most important of all, he's not alone."

Jesse goes to Doggie View Day
30 Care in Los Angeles, California. He plays with other dogs in a large backyard. There is a pool so Jesse can go swimming with the other dogs, too. The day care costs about U.S.
35 $25.00 a day, but Denise is happy to take him there. Denise's neighbors are happy, too. Denise explains, "When Jesse is home alone, he **barks** very loudly all day."

---

1. **Main Idea.** What is the most important idea of the story? Fill in the bubble.

- (A) Day care for dogs is popular in many cities.
- (B) Jesse likes to go swimming with other dogs.
- (C) Denise takes her dog to Doggie View Day Care.

2. Just the Facts. Circle Yes, No, or I don't know.

1. Denise is a dog.   Yes (No) I don't know
2. Jesse is a dog.   Yes No   I don't know
3. Jesse drives to work.   Yes No   I don't know
4. Denise is married.   Yes No   I don't know
5. Jesse enjoys the day care center.   Yes No   I don't know
6. Denise works at a computer company.   Yes No   I don't know
7. Jesse likes to be alone all day.   Yes No   I don't know

3. Learn New Words. Choose the correct words. Write them on the lines.

barks   drives   exercise   gets ready   ~~take~~

1. Jesse and Denise _____ take _____ a walk together.
2. Denise _____ for work after their walk.
3. Denise _____ Jesse to a nearby day care center.
4. He runs around and gets a lot of _____.
5. Jesse _____ loudly at home when he is alone all day.

4. Find the Answers. Use sentences in Activity 3 to answer the questions.

1. What do Denise and Jesse do every morning?
   Jesse and Denise take a walk together. _____

2. What does Jesse do at the day care center?
   _____

3. Where does Denise drive Jesse?
   _____

4. Why does Denise take Jesse to a day care center?
   _____

5. What does Denise do after she takes a walk with Jesse?
   _____

5. **Think It Over.** With a partner, circle the correct answers.

1. Denise is happy to take Jesse to a day care center because _____.
   a. it costs U.S. $25.00
   b. Jesse isn't lonely there
   c. day care for dogs is popular

2. The neighbors are happy when Jesse is at the day care center because _____.
   a. he isn't lonely
   b. he barks all day at home
   c. he can play with other dogs

6. **Talk It Over.** Read the sentences below. Put a check (✓) under the place where Jesse can do these things. Then talk about your answers with your classmates.

SENTENCES	AT HOME	AT DAY CARE	BOTH
1. He plays with other dogs.		✓	
2. He is alone.			
3. He gets exercise.			
4. He barks all day.			
5. He has no one to play with.			
6. He takes a nap.			
7. He goes swimming.			
8. He eats food.			

7. **Write It Down.** Do you think a day care center for pets is a good idea? Why or why not? Complete the sentence and share it with your classmates.

I (think/don't think) this is a good idea because _____

_____

_____

_____

Activity Menu CHAPTERS 1 AND 2

1. **Tie It Together.** With a partner, complete the chart below. Check (✓) the correct person.

	LORI CHEONG	DENISE PEREZ
1. She works all day.	✓	✓
2. She has a small apartment.		
3. She loves dogs.		
4. She has a dog.		
5. She doesn't have a dog.		
6. She likes to play with Princess.		
7. She takes walks with Jesse.		
8. She goes to dog cafés.		
9. She lives in California.		

2. **Write It Down.** Think about Lori and Denise. How are they the same? How are they different? Look at Activity 1 above. Complete the following sentences.

Lori and Denise are the same because _____

_____

_____

Lori and Denise are different because _____

_____

_____

3. **Just For Fun.** Look at the words in the box. With a partner, find and circle the words in the puzzle.

R	L	E	F	A	C	B	T	E	F
E	C	O	D	J	A	D	V	F	A
T	A	O	N	R	B	I	O	Q	V
U	G	N	K	E	S	T	A	C	O
P	E	E	B	N	L	J	K	H	R
M	S	W	E	U	S	Y	U	K	I
O	A	P	A	R	T	M	E	N	T
C	X	E	S	I	C	R	E	X	E
E	P	O	P	U	L	A	R	L	C
R	O	N	P	J	K	N	G	U	D

Word List
- apartment
- bark
- cafe
- cages
- computer
- exercise
- expensive
- favorite
- lonely
- popular

4. **Take a Survey.** Ask six classmates the question below. Complete the chart with their answers.

DO YOU WANT TO HAVE A DOG? WHY?			
Name	**Yes**	**No**	**Reason**
Mari	✓		I love animals.

CHAPTER 3

Double the Fun

Before You Read. Look at the picture and read the title of the story.

1. **Circle your answers and write them on the lines.**

    Double means _____.

    a. one time **b.** two times **c.** three times

    These people work _____.

    a. at a restaurant **b.** at a school **c.** in an office

    These pairs of people look _____.

    a. different **b.** alike **c.** worried

2. **Write your answers on the lines.**

    When you go to a restaurant, who brings your food? _____.

    Do you like to go to restaurants? Why? _____.

Double the Fun

MIKE BING AND HIS WIFE LYNN WERE in a beautiful, new restaurant. A waitress with short, curly hair came to their table. Mike asked her for a cup of
5 tea. A few minutes later, the waitress with short, curly hair came back again. But she did not have Mike's tea. She said to Mike and Lynn, "Do you want something to drink?" Again, Mike asked
10 for a cup of tea. Suddenly, two waitresses came back to the table. They both had a cup of tea for Mike. And they both had short, curly hair. In fact, they looked **exactly** the same. What
15 happened? Mike and Lynn were at Twins Restaurant in New York City.

Lisa and Debbie Ganz are the **owners** of Twins Restaurant. The two women are identical twins. In fact, all
20 the people who work at Twins Restaurant are twins. Thirty-seven **sets** of twins work there, and each set wears the same clothes. Sometimes customers like Mike and Lynn Bing get
25 **confused**. But the restaurant is a lot of fun. Everything at the Twins Restaurant is **double**. For example, there are two doorknobs on each door.

The Ganz sisters are always happy
30 when twins come into the restaurant to eat. The twin guests sign their names in a **special** book. Then the twins can take a picture with the Ganz sisters. Usually the Ganz sisters put
35 these pictures on the walls. There are a lot of pictures of twins on the walls of the restaurant. There are pictures on the walls of famous twins, too. But the Twins Restaurant is not only for twins.
40 It's also for people like Mike and Lynn Bing. But it's double the fun for twins!

---

1. **Main Idea.** **What is the most important idea of the story? Fill in the bubble.**

(A) Twins Restaurant in New York City is an unusual place to eat.

(B) It is fun for twins to visit Twins Restaurant in New York City.

(C) The waitresses at Twins Restaurant in New York City are twins.

2. Just the Facts. Circle the letters of the true sentences.

1. **a.** Mike and Lynn Bing are twins.
   (b.) Debbie and Lisa Ganz are twins.

2. **a.** Mike was confused because there were twin waitresses.
   b. Mike was confused because he asked for a cup of tea.

3. **a.** Only twins can go to Twins Restaurant.
   b. Anyone can go to Twins Restaurant.

4. **a.** Some of the workers at the restaurant are twins.
   b. All of the workers at the restaurant are twins.

5. **a.** There are pictures of twins on the walls of the restaurant.
   b. There are pictures of all the customers on the walls of the restaurant.

6. **a.** Only twins can sign the special book.
   b. All the customers can sign the special book.

3. Learn New Words. Circle the correct words. Write them on the lines.

1. Both waitresses had short, curly hair. They looked _____exactly_____ the same.
   almost   special   (exactly)

2. The restaurant is fun for the _____ who eat there.
   customers   workers   waitresses

3. Sometimes customers like Mike and Lynn Bing get _____ when they see
   identical waiters and waitresses.   confused   double   tired

4. Twins sign their names in a _____ book. It is only for twins.
   small   special   picture

5. Everything at Twins Restaurant is_____. There are two doorknobs on
   each door.   customer   owner   double

6. Lisa and Debbie Ganz are the _____ of Twins Restaurant.
   They enjoy their restaurant.   customers   owners   waitresses

7. Thirty-seven _____ of twins work at Twins Restaurant.
   sets   pictures   kinds

4. Find the Answers. With a partner, use sentences from Activity 3 to answer the questions.

1. Why was Mike confused?
   Both waitresses had short, curly hair. They looked exactly the same.

2. What do twins do when they go to the restaurant?
   _____

3. Who are the Ganz sisters?
   _____

4. Who works at Twins Restaurant?
   _____

5. Complete the Paragraph. Use the words below to complete the paragraph.

both	curly	exactly	happened	~~waitresses~~

   The two (1) _____waitresses_____ came back to the table. They (2) _____ had a cup of tea for Mike. And they both had short, (3) _____ hair. In fact, they looked (4) _____ the same. What (5) _____? The Bings were at Twins Restaurant.

6. Talk It Over. Why is Twins Restaurant unusual? Write three reasons. Then talk about your answers with your classmates.

TWINS RESTAURANT IS UNUSUAL BECAUSE...
there are two doorknobs on each door.

7. Write It Down. Twins Restaurant is a fun place to eat. What is a fun place to eat in a city you know? Write three to four sentences about it.

A fun place to eat is _____. It is fun because _____
_____
_____

The Underwater Hotel

Before You Read. **Look at the picture and read the title of the story.**

1. **Circle your answers and write them on the lines.**

> Where is this woman? She's _____.

> **a.** on land　　　　**b.** underwater　　　　**c.** in space

> This woman is _____.

> **a.** exercising　　　　**b.** scuba diving　　　　**c.** fishing

> She is wearing _____.

> **a.** a bathing suit　　　　**b.** a business suit　　　　**c.** a wet suit

2. **Write your answers on the lines.**

> Why do people go underwater like this? _____.

> Did you ever do this activity? _____.

The Underwater Hotel

LAST YEAR, THE KUBOTA FAMILY took a vacation in Key Largo, Florida, in the U.S. When they arrived, they did not walk or drive to their
5 hotel. They swam to their hotel. The Kubota family went to Jules' Undersea Lodge. This unusual hotel is 21 feet (6.4 meters) underwater.

Jules' Undersea Lodge was not
10 always a hotel. Years ago, it was a laboratory for scientists. The scientists studied fish and plants in the ocean. Two scientists, Neil Monney and Ian Koblick, decided to change the
15 lab into a hotel. The two scientists studied ocean life for many years. They also built underwater labs. They knew that people enjoyed looking at fish, and swimming with them, too.

20 Guests at the lodge must know how to scuba dive before they go to the hotel. The Kubota family didn't know how to dive, so they took a three-hour class first. Then they all
25 put on wet suits. They dove down to the hotel together. Before they entered the lodge, they stopped at the "wet room." There they took off their wet suits and they dried off.
30 Then they entered the hotel.

Jules' Undersea Lodge is not very big. There are two bedrooms, a bathroom, and a living room. There are large windows, a TV, and a
35 telephone. It looks like a regular hotel on the inside, but there are fish outside the windows. Each room in the hotel has large, round windows. Sometimes the fish stop at the
40 windows to look inside!

The Kubota family enjoyed their unusual vacation. They enjoyed watching the fish and swimming with them, too.

1. Main Idea. What is the most important idea of the story? Fill in the bubble.

(A) The Kubota family learned to scuba dive before they went to the hotel.

(B) Jules' Undersea Lodge is an underwater hotel.

(C) Jules' Undersea Lodge looks like a regular hotel on the inside.

2. Just the Facts. Check (✓) True or False.

	True	False
1. Jules' Undersea Lodge is in Key Largo, Florida.	✓	
2. Jules' Undersea Lodge is a laboratory for scientists.		
3. The Kubota family built the underwater hotel.		
4. Some scientists study ocean life.		
5. Jules' Undersea Lodge is a very big hotel.		
6. Guests at Jules' Undersea Lodge can swim with fish.		

3. Learn New Words. Choose the correct word to complete each sentence. Write your answers on the lines.

ago   dive   guests   ~~hotel~~   laboratory   regular   swam

1. Jules' Undersea Lodge is a _____hotel_____ under the water. It has two bedrooms, a bathroom, and a living room.

2. People who stay at a hotel are _____.

3. The Kubota family learned to scuba _____ before they went to the hotel.

4. Jules' Undersea Lodge has bedrooms and a TV like a _____ hotel.

5. Last year, the Kubota family _____ underwater with the fish.

6. Scientists often work in a _____.

7. Jules' Undersea Lodge was not always a hotel. Years _____ it was a laboratory for scientists.

4. Correct the Sentences. The underlined parts of these sentences are wrong. With a partner, rewrite the sentences with the correct information.

1. <u>Key Largo, Florida</u> is 21 feet underwater.
   Jules' Undersea Lodge is 21 feet underwater. _____

2. The two scientists changed the <u>hotel into a lab</u> because people enjoy ocean life.
   _____

3. The Kubota family stopped at the "wet room" <u>to look at the fish.</u>
   _____

4. The lodge looks like a regular hotel <u>on the outside</u>.
   _____

5. The Kubota family didn't know how to dive, so they <u>went home</u>.
   _____

5. **Talk It Over.** Jules' Undersea Lodge is not a regular hotel. Why is it unusual? Write three reasons and talk about them with your classmates.

JULES' UNDERSEA LODGE IS UNUSUAL BECAUSE...
it is underwater.

6. **Think It Over.** Why do some people go to Jules' Undersea Lodge? Share three ideas with your classmates.

SOME PEOPLE GO TO JULES' UNDERSEA LODGE BECAUSE...
they like to see fish.

7. **Write It Down.** Do you want to visit Jules' Undersea Lodge? Why or why not? Write two to three sentences and share them with your classmates.

I (want/don't want) to visit Jules' Undersea Lodge because _____

_____

_____

_____

Activity Menu

1. **Tie It Together.** Think about the places in Chapters 3 and 4. Then complete the chart below with a partner.

	TWINS RESTAURANT	JULES' UNDERSEA LODGE
1. It is an unusual place.	✓	✓
2. People eat there.		
3. People swim there.		
4. It has bedrooms.		
5. It has a bathroom.		
6. Only twins work there.		
7. It has a telephone.		
8. It is underwater.		
9. It is in New York.		
10. It is in the U.S.		

2. **Write It Down.** Think about Twins Restaurant and Jules' Undersea Lodge. How are they similar? How are they different? Complete the chart below.

TWINS RESTAURANT AND JULES' UNDERSEA LODGE	
They are similar because...	**They are different because...**
they are unusual.	the restaurant is in New York and the hotel is in Florida.

3. Just for Fun. Complete the activity with a partner.

a. Unscramble the following sentences.

Example:

people	like	unusual	visit	Some	places	to

Some _people_ _like_ _to_ _visit_ _unusual_ _places_ .

1. Restaurant   have   the   double   Twins   Twins   at   fun

_____ _____ _____ _____ _____ _____ _____ _____ .

2. fish   People   unusual   this   swim   with   hotel   at

_____ _____ _____ _____ _____ _____ _____ _____ .

b. Now write two scrambled sentences. Ask your partner to unscramble them.

1. _____ _____ _____ _____ _____ _____

    _____ _____ _____ _____ _____ _____ .

2. _____ _____ _____ _____ _____ _____

    _____ _____ _____ _____ _____ _____ .

4. Talk It Over. Tell your classmates about an unusual place you know. Then write your answer and your classmates' answers in the chart.

CITY	UNUSUAL PLACE	WHY IS IT UNUSUAL?

5. Go Online. Look at Activity 4 and choose one of the unusual places on the chart. Use an Internet search engine like Google and type in the name of the place. Find a Web site for that place and write the Web address here.

_____

CHAPTER 5

Circus Family

Before You Read. Look at the picture and read the title of the story.

1. **Circle your answers and write them on the lines.**

   The people are _____.

   a. teachers　　　　　　**b.** doctors　　　　　　**c.** clowns

   They work at a _____.

   a. restaurant　　　　　　**b.** circus　　　　　　**c.** hotel

2. **What can you see at the circus? Circle the things you can see there.**

THINGS YOU SEE AT THE CIRCUS			
1. elephants	3. fish	5. dancers	7. jugglers
2. clowns	4. cars	6. horses	8. movies

3. **Write your answers on the lines.**

   Did you ever go to a circus? _____ Where? _____

Circus Family

WHEN JON WEISS GETS READY FOR his job, he puts on make-up, a large red nose, and big striped shoes. His wife, Laura, laughs at his **costume**.
5 Everyone at work laughs at it, too, but Jon loves his job. Jon is a **clown** in the **circus**. Sometimes his job is **dangerous** because Jon is a "human cannonball." First, he climbs into a cannon. A cannon
10 is like a very large gun. Then someone **pushes** a button on the cannon. Jon **shoots** 120 feet (36.6 meters) out of the cannon every night at the circus. Is Jon's wife **worried**? No. In fact, she
15 pushes the button.

Jon and Laura met when they were in high school. Jon's classmates always laughed at Jon because he was very funny. He liked to make people laugh,
20 so he went to work at the circus after he graduated. Laura went with him. Jon and Laura wanted to stay in the circus for a year before they went to college. But they both really enjoyed the circus,
25 so they decided to stay.

The couple now has three children. They all travel around the country together with the circus. Their oldest child, Jonny, is seven years old.
30 Sometimes he works in the circus, too. He wears a clown costume, like his father. Jon and Jonny drive around the circus together in a miniature car, and Jonny waves to all the people. When
35 Jonny is busy, his little sister, four-year-old Nicole, drives with Jon in the small car. Their little brother, Max, is only two years old. He is still too young to be in the circus. Jon and Laura think
40 the circus is a wonderful place for their family. They spend a lot of time together, and the children have fun, too.

---

1. **Main Idea.** **What is the most important idea of the story? Fill in the bubble.**

- Ⓐ The Weiss family enjoys being together in the circus.
- Ⓑ Jon Weiss started to work for the circus after high school.
- Ⓒ Jon Weiss likes to make people laugh.

2. Just the Facts. Circle Yes, No, or I don't know.

1. Is Jon Weiss a clown?   (Yes)   No   I don't know
2. Is Laura worried about Jon?   Yes   No   I don't know
3. Did Jon's father work at the circus?   Yes   No   I don't know
4. Did Jon graduate from high school?   Yes   No   I don't know
5. Did Jon and Laura go to college?   Yes   No   I don't know
6. Do their children go to school?   Yes   No   I don't know
7. Does Jon enjoy his job?   Yes   No   I don't know
8. Does Max work at the circus?   Yes   No   I don't know
9. Does Jon spend a lot of time with his family?   Yes   No   I don't know

3. Learn New Words. Choose the correct words. Write them on the lines.

circus   clown   ~~costume~~   dangerous   pushes   shoots   worried

1. Jon puts on make-up, a red nose, and big striped shoes. That is his _____costume_____.
2. Jon is a _____ in the circus.
3. Jon works at the _____. It's a fun place to work.
4. Sometimes his job is _____ because Jon is a "human cannonball."
5. He climbs into a cannon, and someone _____ a button on the cannon.
6. Jon _____ 120 feet out of the cannon every night at the circus.
7. Laura isn't _____ about Jon because she pushes the button on the cannon.

4. Find the Answers. Answer the questions with a partner.

1. Why did Jon go to work at the circus?
   He went to work at the circus because _____

2. How long did Jon and Laura want to stay in the circus before college?

   _____

3. Why did they stay in the circus?

   _____

5. **Think It Over.** Jon and Laura Weiss think the circus is a good place for their children. But some people do not agree. Think about some reasons for both opinions. Write the reasons below, and share them with your classmates.

THE CIRCUS IS A GOOD PLACE FOR CHILDREN BECAUSE...	THE CIRCUS IS NOT A GOOD PLACE FOR CHILDREN BECAUSE...
they can be with their family.	they can't live in a house.

6. **Take a Survey.** Ask your classmates this question. Count their answers and put the numbers in the chart.

QUESTION	YES	NO
Do you think the circus is a good place for Jon and Laura's children?		

7. **Write It Down.** Jon and Laura Weiss think the circus is a wonderful place for their family. Do you agree with them? Why or why not? Write three to four sentences and share them with your classmates.

I (agree/disagree) with Jon and Laura because _____

_____

_____

_____

CHAPTER 6

The Thrill of It

Before You Read. Look at the picture and read the title of the story.

1. **Circle your answers and write them on the lines.**

   This is _____.

   a. an elevator   **b.** a roller coaster   **c.** a toy

   Where is it? It's in _____.

   a. an amusement park   **b.** a hotel   **c.** a backyard

2. **Write your answers on the lines.**

   Did you ever go on a ride like this? _____.

   People go on rides like this because _____.

The Thrill of It

ROLLER COASTERS ARE POPULAR all over the world. In fact, some people will wait in line for hours to ride a roller coaster. At Fujikyu
5 Highland Park in Fujiyoshida, Japan, Yosuke Kawase waited **in line** for four and a half hours to ride Dodonpa, the fastest roller coaster in the world. Yosuke says, "I love roller coasters
10 because of the **thrill** and the **speed**. I don't **mind** waiting in line." John Ivers lives thousands of miles away from Yosuke and he loves roller coasters, too. But he hates to wait in line. So he
15 built a roller coaster in his backyard!

John lives in Bruceville, Indiana, in the U.S. He is an engineer. He and his wife, Sharon, have two daughters and four grandchildren. John built his
20 roller coaster, the Blue Flash, a few years ago. It is 20 feet (about six meters) high. It **travels** over John's barn, and around an elm tree. It goes about 25 miles (about 40 kilometers)
25 per hour. Yosuke paid 1,000 yen (U.S. $7.75) for a one-minute ride on Dodonpa. The Blue Flash is a much shorter ride. It takes only eleven seconds, but the ride is free for the
30 Ivers family. Most important of all, they never have to wait in line.

Now John is **busy** again. He is building another roller coaster. This one will travel around his garden. He
35 says it will be bigger, faster, and better than the Blue Flash.

John is excited about his new roller coaster. But not everyone enjoys roller coasters. John's wife,
40 Sharon, doesn't. She thinks they're dangerous. She is afraid of heights and will not get on the Blue Flash.

---

1. **Main Idea.** What is the most important idea of the story? Fill in the bubble.

- Ⓐ Yosuke Kawase likes to wait in line to ride Dodonpa.
- Ⓑ Many people love to ride roller coasters.
- Ⓒ John Ivers built a roller coaster in his backyard.

2. Just the Facts. Circle the letters of the correct sentences.

1. **a.** Roller coasters are only popular in Japan and the U.S.
   (b.) Roller coasters are very popular all over the world.

2. **a.** Dodonpa is in Indiana.
   b. The Blue Flash is in Indiana.

3. **a.** John Ivers hates to wait in line.
   b. Yosuke Kawase hates to wait in line.

4. **a.** John's wife loves to ride the Blue Flash.
   b. John's wife is afraid to ride the Blue Flash.

5. **a.** John Ivers is an engineer.
   b. Yosuke Kawase is an engineer.

6. **a.** John's family loves to build roller coasters.
   b. John's family loves to ride his roller coaster.

3. Learn New Words. Circle the correct words. Write them on the lines.

1. Some people wait _____in line_____ for hours to ride on a roller coaster.
   around (in line) outside

2. The Blue Flash is not very fast. The _____ is 25 miles per hour.
   speed   height   thrill

3. Yosuke waited for four and a half hours. He doesn't _____ waiting in line.
   like   choose   mind

4. Yosuke loves the _____ of roller coasters. They're very exciting.
   thrill   cost   busy

5. John's roller coaster _____ over his barn and around a tree.
   drives   travels   speed

6. John is _____ again. He is building another roller coaster.
   busy   riding   in line

4. **Talk It Over.** With a partner, put the sentences in the correct places in the chart below. Talk about your answers with your classmates.

~~It takes one minute.~~   ~~It takes eleven seconds.~~

John Ivers built it.   It is in Japan.

It is in the U.S.   It's the fastest roller coaster in the world.

Yosuke Kawase rode it.   It travels around a barn.

A ride costs U.S. $7.75.   A ride is free.

THE BLUE FLASH	DODONPA
1. It takes eleven seconds.	1. It takes one minute.
2.	2.
3.	3.
4.	4.
5.	5.

5. **Think It Over.** Read the questions below. Talk about your answers with a group, and write them on the lines.

1. Why did John Ivers build the Blue Flash?

He built it because _____

2. Why do you think John Ivers is building another roller coaster?

_____

6. **Write It Down.** Complete the following sentences.

1. John Ivers and Yosuke Kawase are similar because _____

_____

2. John Ivers and Yosuke Kawase are different because _____

_____

7. **Take a Survey.** Ask your classmates this question. Count their answers and put the numbers on the chart.

QUESTION	YES	NO
Do you like to ride roller coasters?		

Activity Menu

1. **Tie It Together.** With a partner, write each word in the correct point on the star below. Then add more words from Chapters 5 and 6.

afraid	cannon	costume	fun	ride
backyard	children	daughter	grandchildren	thrill
Bruceville	circus	family	hate	travel
build	~~clown~~	Fujiyoshida	love	worried

More words:

_____ _____ _____ _____

Places

Things   clown   People

Activities   Feelings

2. **Go Online.** The oldest roller coaster in the world is called Leap-the-Dips. Where is it? How old is it? Use an Internet search engine like Google and type in "Leap-the-Dips."

Leap-the-Dips is in _____. It is _____ years old.

3. **Talk It Over.** How are John Ivers and Jon Weiss similar? How are the two men different? Write your answers in the chart, then share them with your classmates.

JOHN IVERS AND JON WEISS	
How are they similar?	**How are they different?**
They are both married.	John Ivers is an engineer.

4. **Write It Down.** You are the son or daughter of Jon Weiss or John Ivers. Write three to four sentences about your unusual father.

My father is _____. He _____

_____

_____

_____

5. **Just for Fun.** Find and circle the words.

D	S	U	C	R	I	C	P	L	E
B	A	V	A	C	K	W	P	E	N
U	S	N	Y	F	N	V	W	V	G
S	L	G	G	W	Y	O	Z	A	I
Y	P	L	O	E	R	Y	X	R	N
V	Z	L	I	R	R	M	S	T	E
P	C	I	I	R	P	O	K	C	E
S	P	E	E	D	H	U	U	I	R
E	D	I	S	H	P	T	S	S	F
L	I	C	U	P	S	W	H	H	V

Word List
busy
circus
clown
dangerous
~~engineer~~
push
speed
thrill
travel
worried

CHAPTER 7

A Race to Get Married

Before You Read. Look at the picture and read the title of the story.

1. **Write your answers on the lines.**

    Look at the picture. This is a _____.

    Why do some people do this? _____

    The people in this story will _____.

2. **Circle your answer and complete this sentence.**

    I (like/don't like) to run because _____.

A Race to Get Married

ON SATURDAY, APRIL 7, WANDA JOHNS, 49, and Clarence Melion, 56, ran a five-kilometer race in Valparaiso, Indiana, in the U.S. This was not
5 unusual for them. They both enjoy running and sometimes run in **marathons**, too. They both **belong** to the same running club and met at a race four years ago. But Saturday's
10 race was a little different. When they finished the race, Wanda and Clarence got married.

During a race last year, Clarence asked Wanda to marry him. Wanda said
15 "Yes," but they didn't know where to get married. Many of their friends are in the same running club. Clarence and Wanda decided to get married at a race so their friends could be with them.
20 They both wore shorts, T-shirts, and running shoes at their wedding. Wanda also wore a white veil on her baseball cap.

Clarence usually runs five
25 kilometers (about three miles) in about 25 minutes. Wanda usually runs the same **distance** in about 27 minutes. But on Saturday, they ran the race together. They were almost finished when
30 Wanda's hat **blew off**. She **continued** to run, but Clarence ran back to pick up her hat. He picked it up and followed her to the finish line. Together they finished the race in about 33 minutes.
35 Then they got married.

Hundreds of runners watched Wanda and Clarence's wedding. When it was over, everyone clapped for the couple. Then they all ate pizza and
40 fruit. Wanda's son, Brian, was not surprised at the unusual wedding. He said, "They both love to run and to race. It's perfect."

1. Main Idea. What is the most important idea of the story? Fill in the bubble.

(A) Wanda and Clarence got married after a race.

(B) Wanda and Clarence met at a race a few years ago.

(C) Wanda and Clarence run in races and marathons.

2. Just the Facts. Circle the letters of the correct sentences.

1. **a.** Wanda usually runs faster than Clarence.
   (b.) Clarence usually runs faster than Wanda.
2. **a.** Clarence and Wanda met at a race four years ago.
   b. Clarence and Wanda got married at a race four years ago.
3. **a.** Wanda wore a white veil on her baseball cap.
   b. They both wore white veils on their baseball caps.
4. **a.** Wanda dropped her cap and stopped running.
   b. Wanda dropped her cap and continued running.
5. **a.** Hundreds of runners watched the race.
   b. Hundreds of runners watched the wedding.

3. Learn New Words. Choose the correct words. Write them on the lines.

~~belong~~   blew off   continued   distance   marathons

1. Wanda and Clarence _____belong_____ to the same running club.
2. They both enjoy running. They sometimes run in _____.
3. Wanda's hat _____. It fell onto the street.
4. Wanda _____ to run. She didn't stop to pick up her hat.
5. Clarence runs five kilometers in about 25 minutes. Wanda usually runs the same _____ in about 27 minutes.

4. Correct the Sentences. The underlined parts of these sentences are wrong. With a partner, rewrite the sentences with the correct information.

1. Everyone clapped because Wanda and Clarence <u>finished the race</u>.
   <u>Everyone clapped because Wanda and Clarence got married.</u>
2. They decided to get married at a race so <u>they could eat pizza and fruit</u>.
   _____
3. Saturday's race was <u>the same as all races</u>.
   _____
4. Clarence <u>dropped</u> the hat and followed Wanda to the finish line.
   _____
5. <u>A few people</u> watched Wanda and Clarence's wedding.
   _____

5. Finish the Sentences. With a partner, draw lines from the words on the left to the words on the right to complete the sentences.

1. Clarence asked Wanda to marry him
2. Wanda and Clarence got married
3. Wanda's hat blew off
4. Everyone clapped for the couple
5. Wanda's son, Brian, was not surprised

a. when they finished Saturday's race.
b. when they were almost finished.
c. that Wanda got married at the race.
d. during a race last year.
e. when the wedding was over.

6. Talk It Over. Do you think it's a good idea to get married at a race? Why or why not? Write your answer on the lines and talk about it with your classmates.

I think it (is/isn't) a good idea because _____

_____

_____

7. Write It Down. Why was Saturday's race unusual? Write three to four sentences.

Saturday's race was unusual because _____

_____

_____

_____

CHAPTER 8

Married with Two Homes

Before You Read. Look at the picture and read the title of the story.

1. Write three questions about the people in the picture. After you read the story, answer the questions.

QUESTIONS	ANSWERS
Example: Are the people happy?	Yes, they are.
1.	1.
2.	2.
3.	3.

2. Write your answer on the line.

Do you live with your family? _____.

Married with Two Homes

JOSEPH AND LIZ STEVENS ARE happily married. They have two children. But they do not all live together. In fact, they live in different
5 states in the U.S. Joseph lives in Illinois, and Liz lives with the children, Ben and Judy, in Indiana. Their homes are 336 miles (about 540 km) apart. Joseph and Liz do not see each other
10 every week, but they talk on the phone every day.

Joseph and Liz got married 20 years ago. For **most** of their marriage, they lived together in Indiana. Liz
15 worked for a university near their home, and Joseph worked for an **airline** company. But Joseph's company moved to Illinois about four years ago, and Joseph went with it.
20 Liz didn't want to leave her job and move to Illinois. The children, Ben and Judy, didn't want to leave their schools. So now the family lives **apart**. They see each other about five
25 days every month. Joseph can fly free to visit his wife and children because he works for an airline. But the telephone calls are **expensive**! Sometimes their telephone **bill** is U.S.
30 $500 for one month.

Many married couples in the U.S., like the Stevens, do not live together. In fact, about one million couples live apart. Work is usually the **reason**. But
35 it is not easy to have two homes. First of all, it is very expensive. Second of all, it is sometimes lonely. Joseph says, "I often miss my wife and children, but Ben and Judy are happy. They know
40 we love them, so it doesn't matter where we live." Joseph and Liz want to live together again when the children finish school. But one of them will need to get a new job.

1. Main Idea. What is the most important idea of the story? Fill in the bubble.

(A) It is very expensive to make a telephone call to Indiana.

(B) Liz and Joseph are married, but they live in different states.

(C) The Stevens family wants to live together again soon.

2. Just the Facts. Circle the correct words. Write them on the lines.

1. Liz and Joseph Stevens live _____ apart _____ .
   together (apart) in Indiana

2. The couple lived together _____ their marriage.
   before   until   in the beginning of

3. The two children live with their _____ .
   mother   father   classmates

4. Their telephone bill is _____ .
   free   cheap   expensive

5. Joseph does not pay to fly because he works _____ .
   for free   five days a month   for an airline

6. Ben and Judy go to school in _____ .
   Indiana   Illinois   Florida

7. Liz and Joseph will live together again when the children _____ .
   finish school   grow up   get jobs

3. Learn New Words. Circle the words that have the same meaning as the underlined words.

1. For most of their marriage, Joseph and Liz lived together in Indiana.
   (more than half of)   about half of

2. Ben and Judy are happy and they know their parents love them. So it doesn't matter where they live.
   isn't important   isn't far from

3. Joseph and Liz want to live together when the children finish school.
   start   complete

4. About one million couples live apart. Work is usually the reason.
   cause   job

4. **Complete the Paragraph.** Use the words below to complete the paragraph.

airline   ~~apart~~   bill   expensive   free

    The Stevens family lives (1) _____apart_____. Joseph can fly (2) _____ to visit his wife and children because he works for an (3) _____. But the telephone calls are (4) _____! Their telephone (5) _____ is sometimes U.S. $500 for one month.

5. **Think It Over.** Many married couples in the United States do not live together. Work is usually the reason. What are some other reasons? Write three more reasons in the chart and share them with a partner.

REASONS	
work	

6. **Talk It Over.** Write your answers on the lines. Then talk about them with a group.

1. Does Joseph Stevens think it is easy to have two homes? _____

2. Why or why not? _____

_____

_____

7. **Write It Down.** Pretend that you are Liz or Joseph. Complete the sentences below.

I am (Liz/Joseph). I (like/don't like) to live apart from my (husband/wife) because _____

_____

_____

_____

Activity Menu

1. **Tie It Together.** Look at the words below. Which words go with Chapter 7? Chapter 8? Both? With a partner, write them on the diagram below. Then add more words from the chapters.

~~airline~~	husband	~~married~~	together
apart	Illinois	race	university
club	Indiana	runners	unusual
finish line	~~marathon~~	school	wife

More words:

_____ _____ _____ _____

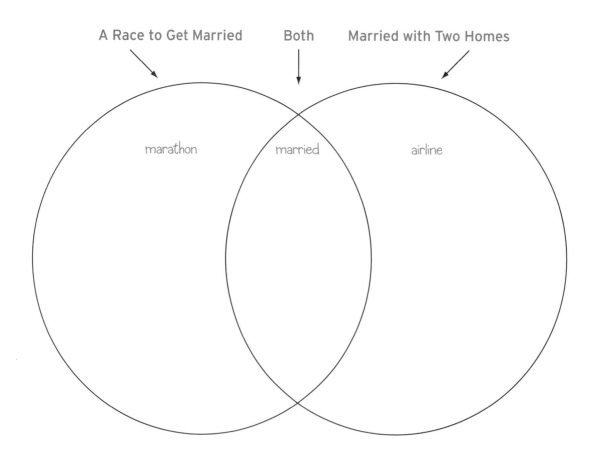

A Race to Get Married   Both   Married with Two Homes

marathon   married   airline

2. **Write It Down.** Think about the two stories in the chapters. Then complete the following sentences.

1. Liz and Joseph's marriage is unusual because _____

   _____

2. Wanda and Clarence's wedding was unusual because _____

   _____

3. **Just for Fun.** Use the clues in the box to complete the puzzle.

Clues

Across
3. ~~college~~
4. take a plane
6. not together
7. run behind someone
10. people who run

Down
1. a long race
2. not the same
5. not cheap
8. do a job

4. **Talk It Over.** Wanda and Clarence enjoy running. What activities do you enjoy? Make a list and talk about it with a group.

ACTIVITIES	
listening to music	

CHAPTER 9

Dream On

Before You Read. Look at the picture and read the title of the story.

1. **Circle your answers and write them on the lines.**

   This person is _____.

   a. thinking   **b.** walking   **c.** sleeping

   People sometimes _____ when they sleep.

   a. eat   **b.** dream   **c.** work

   Do you dream at night?_____.

   a. Yes   **b.** No   **c.** Sometimes

2. **Complete the sentence.**

   What do you dream about?

   I dream about _____

Dream On

STACY TYLER HAD A **PROBLEM**. SHE
wanted to go to college, but she was
not **sure** where she wanted to go. She
was confused. Did she want to go to
5 college near her home and stay with her
friends? Or did she want to go to college
in a different country and leave all her
friends? She thought about her problem
every day. She thought about it every
10 evening, too. One night, Stacy thought
about her problem before she went to
sleep. When she woke up the next
morning, she knew the answer. She knew
where she wanted to go to school. Stacy
15 found the **solution** in her dreams.

Is this unusual? Many doctors say
"No." Dr. Gayle Delaney says that when
we sleep, we can use our dreams to
help us. Everyone has dreams every
20 night. But sometimes we don't
remember our dreams. Dr. Delaney
teaches people how to remember
dreams. Then they can sometimes find
answers to their problems. This is how
25 to do it:

1. Choose a problem to dream about.
2. Write some sentences about your
   problem on a piece of paper and
   keep the paper by your bed.
30 3. Think about your problem as you fall
   asleep. Don't think about other
   things.
4. When you wake up, write your
   dream on a piece of paper.
35 5. Think about your dream very
   carefully. Try to understand your
   dream.

That night, Stacy dreamed she
was in a **strange** room with other
40 people. All the other people spoke
different languages, but Stacy wasn't
afraid. She was very **excited** and happy
to be in a new place with new people.
After this dream, Stacy knew what to
45 do. What do you think she did?

---

1. **Main Idea.** **What is the most important idea of the story? Fill in the bubble.**

- (A) Our dreams can help us solve our problems.
- (B) Stacy Tyler wants to go to college near her home.
- (C) Dr. Delaney teaches people to remember dreams.

2. Just the Facts. Circle Yes, No, or I don't know.

1. Stacy was not sure about where to go to college.   (Yes)   No   I don't know
2. Stacy only thought about her problem at night.   Yes   No   I don't know
3. Stacy's parents wanted her to go to college near home.   Yes   No   I don't know
4. Stacy decided to go to college near her home.   Yes   No   I don't know
5. Stacy decided to go to college in a different country.   Yes   No   I don't know
6. Stacy dreamed about her problem.   Yes   No   I don't know
7. Dr. Delaney teaches people about colleges.   Yes   No   I don't know
8. We don't always remember our dreams.   Yes   No   I don't know
9. Stacy will study French at her college.   Yes   No   I don't know

3. Learn New Words. Choose the correct words. Write them on the lines.

carefully   excited   problem   solution   ~~strange~~   sure

1. Stacy dreamed she was in a _____strange_____ room. She did not know the people in the room.
2. Stacy had a _____. She needed to find the answer.
3. The answer was in Stacy's dream. It was the _____ to her problem.
4. Stacy did not know where to go to college. She was not _____ what to do.
5. In Stacy's dream, she was very _____ and happy to be with new people.
6. When Stacy woke up, she thought about her dream very _____.

4. What Happened First? Don't look at the story. Put the sentences in the correct order. Then look at the story to check your answers.

____ **a.** Think about your problem as you fall asleep. Don't think about other things.

____ **b.** Think about your dream very carefully. Try to understand your dream.

____ **c.** Write some sentences about your problem on a piece of paper and keep the paper by your bed.

_1_ **d.** Choose a problem to dream about.

____ **e.** When you wake up, write your dream on a piece of paper.

5. **Talk It Over.** Write your answers on the lines. Then talk about them with a partner.

1. What was Stacy's problem?

   Stacy didn't know

2. How did Stacy solve her problem?

3. Where did Stacy decide to go to college?

6. **Write It Down.** Think about a problem that you have. Complete the first two steps on the chart below. Try to solve your problem in your dreams.

MY PROBLEM
1. Choose a problem:
2. Write two to three sentences about your problem:

7. **Take a Survey.** Ask your classmates this question. Count their answers and put the numbers on the chart.

QUESTION	YES	NO
Do your dreams help you solve problems?		

CHAPTER 10

Remember to Sleep

Before You Read. Look at the picture and read the title of the story.

Write your answers on the lines.

What is this woman doing? _____

Does she look sleepy or awake? _____

Do you like to study alone or with friends? _____

Where do you like to study? _____

When do you like to study? _____

Remember to Sleep

ELLEN SIMS IS AN 18 YEAR-OLD college student. She has an important history exam tomorrow morning. Ellen is going to study **all**
5 **night**. She is not going to sleep **at all**. Many college students, like Ellen, do this often. They think that they can study all night. And they think that in the morning, they will remember
10 everything that they studied the night before. Ellen thinks that this is a good way to study, but many doctors disagree. They say that sleep is very important for memory and
15 brain development.

Scientists at Harvard Medical School in the U.S. studied sleep and memory. They studied 24 people. First, they asked the people to look at a
20 picture and **remember** it. At night, they put the people in two groups of 12. Group 1 went to sleep. Group 2 did not. A few days later, the scientists showed some pictures to both groups. They
25 asked the people to find the picture they saw before. The people in Group 1 did well. But the people in Group 2 did not do well. It wasn't easy for them to remember the picture. What
30 happened? Scientists say that sleep helps our memory. After we learn something new, sleep helps us remember it. And when we don't sleep, we can **forget** new things.
35 Scientists say that many teenagers, like Ellen, sleep **too little**. They go to school and they work, too. They also spend time with their friends. They're always busy and they think that sleep
40 doesn't matter. But scientists say the brains of teenagers are still **developing**, and sleep is a very important part of the development. When teens sleep less than six hours, they can't think
45 clearly. That is not very helpful for a student who is taking an exam.

---

1. **Main Idea.** What is the most important idea of the story? Fill in the bubble.

- Ⓐ Sleep helps our memory and brain development.
- Ⓑ Many college students stay up all night to study and don't sleep.
- Ⓒ Doctors showed a picture to 24 people they were studying.

2. Just the Facts. Check (✓) True or False. If a sentence is false, change it to make it true.

	True	False
1. Ellen slept well the night before the history exam.	☐	☑

Ellen did not sleep the night before the history exam.

	True	False
2. Many college students don't sleep at all before exams.	☐	☐
3. There were 24 people in each group in the study.	☐	☐
4. The two groups looked at a picture.	☐	☐
5. Both groups went to sleep that night.	☐	☐
6. A few days later, everyone did well.	☐	☐

3. Learn New Words. Choose the correct words. Write them on the lines.

~~all night~~   a lot   at all   developing   development   forget   remember   too little

1. Sometimes college students stay awake and study _____*all night*_____. They don't

sleep _____ the night before an exam.

2. Sleep is important. When we learn something new, sleep helps us _____ it.

When we don't sleep, we can _____ new things.

3. Many teenagers are very busy. They sleep _____. They don't have

_____ of time to sleep.

4. Ellen is young and her brain is still _____. Sleep is an important part of

her brain's _____.

4. **Talk It Over.** In a group, talk about the sentences below. Which group does each sentence describe? Put a check (✓) in the correct column.

SENTENCES	GROUP 1	GROUP 2
1. This group looked at a picture.	✓	✓
2. This group went to sleep that night.		
3. This group did not go to sleep that night.		
4. The people in this group could not remember the picture very easily a few days later.		
5. The people in this group did well a few days later.		

5. **Write It Down.** Choose Group 1 or Group 2 from Activity 4. Pretend that you are in that group. Write a paragraph. Describe what happened in your group.

_____ I was in Group _____. This is what happened. First _____

_____

_____

_____

6. **Think It Over.** Look at the question below. Circle your answer. Then write your reasons. Share your answer with a partner.

Do you think Ellen did well on her history exam?   Yes   No

I think she (did/didn't do) well because _____

_____

7. **Take a Survey.** How many hours do you sleep at night? Ask five classmates. Write your classmates' names and answers in the chart. Who sleeps the most?

NAME	NUMBER OF HOURS	NAME	NUMBER OF HOURS
Susan	7		

Activity Menu CHAPTERS 9 AND 10

1. **Tie It Together.** With a partner, complete the chart below. Check (✓) the correct person.

	STACY TYLER	ELLEN SIMS
1. She is a college student.		✓
2. She wants to go to college.		
3. She had an important history test.		
4. She studied all night.		
5. She had an important problem.		
6. She went to sleep that night.		
7. She dreamed about her problem.		
8. She didn't sleep the night before the test.		

2. **Think It Over.** In Chapters 9 and 10, doctors say that sleep is important for different reasons. What are the reasons in each chapter? Write your answers. Then share them with your classmates.

WHY IS SLEEP IMPORTANT?	
Chapter 9: Dream On	It is important because
Chapter 10: Remember to Sleep	It is important because

3. **Write It Down.** How much do you sleep? Do you think you need more sleep? Why or why not? Complete the sentences.

I sleep _____ hours every night. I (need/don't need) more sleep because _____

_____

_____

4. **Just for Fun.** Complete the activity with a partner.

a. Unscramble the following sentences.

Example:

our   use   We   us   to   can   dreams   help

___We___ ___can___ ___use___ ___our___ ___dreams___ ___to___ ___help___ ___us___.

1. problem   Stacy   dreams   in   her   solved   her

_____ _____ _____ _____ _____ _____ _____.

2. do   test   students   not   before   Some   a   sleep

_____ _____ _____ _____ _____ _____ _____ _____.

b. Now write two scrambled sentences. Ask your partner to unscramble them.

1. _____ _____ _____ _____ _____ _____

_____ _____ _____ _____ _____.

2. _____ _____ _____ _____ _____ _____

_____ _____ _____ _____ _____.

5. **Go Online.** Dr. Gayle Delaney wrote many books about dreams. Use an Internet search engine like Google and type in "Dr. Gayle Delaney." Find the title of one of her books. Write it here:

_____

CHAPTER 11

A Healthy Choice

Before You Read. Look at the picture and read the title of the story.

1. **Circle your answer and write it on the line.**

    This is a picture of a high school _____.

    a. library   **b.** cafeteria   **c.** gym

2. **What can students buy in a cafeteria? Write some things in the chart.**

THINGS STUDENTS CAN BUY IN A CAFETERIA	
sandwiches	

3. **Complete the sentence.**

    I usually eat _____ for lunch.

A Healthy Choice

THE CAFETERIA AT FREMONT HIGH School in California, in the U.S., is a little different these days. There are no soft drinks or potato chips in the
5 **cafeteria**. The candy bars and ice cream are gone, too. What happened? The school **stopped** selling junk food. The principal and teachers are happy about this. But some students are not.
10 Dana Alvarez is a student at Fremont High School and she is angry. She says, "I like to have soda and chips for lunch. It's not **fair** that I can't **choose** the food I like." But the
15 principal and teachers at this large California school disagree with Dana. In the U.S., 14% of **teenagers** are **overweight**. Doctors say that junk food is one reason for this problem.
20 Sometimes children eat junk food because it is easy to buy. Junk food, like ice cream, chips, and candy, has a lot of fat and sugar. Children eat too much of it, and that is why they are
25 overweight. In addition, teachers say that when children eat junk food for lunch, they often feel sleepy in the afternoon. Many parents are worried, too. They want their children to eat
30 well, and they want the schools to sell only healthy foods.

The cafeteria at Fremont High School sells a lot of different food now, **such as** fruit, yogurt, salads, and juice.
35 But this may not solve the problem. Sometimes students go outside school to buy junk food at lunchtime. And some students bring junk food from home. But in the cafeteria, students
40 may buy only healthy food. The principal hopes that most of his students will make a healthy choice.

1. **Main Idea.** What is the most important idea of the story? Fill in the bubble.

(A) Dana Alvarez wants to have chips and soda for lunch everyday.

(B) The cafeteria at Fremont High School does not sell junk food anymore.

(C) The principal at Fremont High School likes to eat healthy food.

2. Just the Facts. Check (✓) True or False. If a sentence is false, change it to make it true.

	True	False
1. In the U.S., most teenagers are overweight.	☐	✓

In the U.S, 14% of teenagers are overweight.

2. Dana Alverez can buy soda and chips in the cafeteria. ☐ ☐

_____

3. The principal wants the school to sell only healthy food. ☐ ☐

_____

4. Fruit, yogurt, and salads are junk food. ☐ ☐

_____

5. Children who eat junk food are tired before lunch. ☐ ☐

_____

6. Some children bring junk food to school. ☐ ☐

_____

3. Learn New Words. Circle the correct words. Write them on the lines.

1. The students at Fremont High School can't buy candy because the school

_____stopped_____ selling junk food.

(stopped) started is

2. Dana says, "It's not _____ that I can't choose the food I like." Dana wants

overweight fair fun

to have chips and soda for lunch, but she can't.

3. Many _____ in the U.S. are overweight because they eat junk food.

teachers principals teenagers

Junk food makes these students unhealthy.

4. Students sometimes go outside the school at _____ to buy junk food.

home lunchtime work

5. The cafeteria sells different food now, _____ fruit and salads.

such as usually choose

4. **Complete the Sentences.** Use the pairs of words to complete the sentences.

1. gone   ~~cafeteria~~

There are no soft drinks or potato chips in the Fremont High School _____*cafeteria*_____.
The candy bars and ice cream are _____ too.

2. overweight   reason

In the U.S., 14% of teenagers are _____. Doctors say that junk food is one
_____ for this problem.

3. solve   choose

Students at Fremont High School can _____ only healthy food in the
cafeteria. But this may not _____ the problem.

5. **Think It Over.** With a partner, put each word in the correct place on the chart.
Then add other food to the chart.

~~candy bars~~   ~~fruit~~   juice   soft drinks   chips   ice cream   salad   yogurt

JUNK FOOD		HEALTHY FOOD	
candy bars		fruit	

6. **Talk It Over.** The cafeteria at Fremont High School does not sell junk food.
Who thinks this is a good idea? Put a check (✓) in the correct column for each
person, and write the reason. Then talk about your answers with your classmates.

PEOPLE	IT'S A GOOD IDEA.	IT'S A BAD IDEA.	REASON
1. Dana Alvarez		✓	She can't choose the food she likes.
2. The teachers			
3. Doctors			

7. **Write It Down.** Choose Dana, the teachers, or doctors from Activity 6. Write why
you agree or disagree with them.

I (agree/disagree) with _____ because _____

_____

CHAPTER 12

Fun, Fit, and Free

Before You Read. Look at the picture and read the title of the story.

1. **Circle your answers.**

   What are these people doing?

   a. dancing   **b.** exercising   **c.** working

   Why are they doing this?

   a. for their jobs   **b.** for their health   **c.** for money

   Where are these people?

   a. at home   **b.** at work   **c.** at a gym

2. **Write your answer on the line.**

   Did you go to a place like this? _____

Fun, Fit, and Free

TWO YEARS AGO, JOHN STREET READ a story in an American magazine, and he **became** very unhappy. The story said that Philadelphia, Pennsylvania,
5 was the fattest city in the U.S. Why was John unhappy about this? He was the mayor of Philadelphia, and he was worried about his city.

When John Street was young, he
10 was very overweight. His doctor said this was unhealthy. John needed to lose weight, so he started to exercise and eat well. Slowly, he lost 60 pounds and felt great! He **continued** to exercise
15 and eat the right food to stay healthy. Mayor Street knew that he could help the people of Philadelphia lose weight and get fit, too. He thought, "Then we will be a better city, and our citizens
20 will feel better. Philadelphia will be a healthier place to live."

Mayor Street started a new **program** called Fun, Fit, and Free to help Philadelphians have fun, become
25 fit, and be free from fat. The program **encourages** people to eat healthy food, exercise every day, and drink **plenty of** water. Philadelphians can go to the Fun, Fit, and Free Web site to join. About
30 30,000 people are in the program. When they lose weight, they write stories online to tell about it. This encourages other people to lose weight. There is information on the Web site
35 about how to eat healthy food, too.

Many businesses in Philadelphia are also helping. Some restaurants now offer more choices of healthy food. Health clubs are open in the afternoon, so
40 people can exercise at lunchtime. Some Philadelphia hospitals have free classes to teach people about good health. Fun, Fit, and Free is very successful so far. The people of Philadelphia lost a
45 total of six tons (about 5,443 kilos) in two years. Philadelphia is **no longer** the fattest city in the U.S., and John Street is very happy.

1. **Main Idea.** What is the most important idea of the story? Fill in the bubble.

- (A) Mayor John Street lost 60 pounds when he was a young man.
- (B) Mayor John Street wants Philadelphians to be healthy.
- (C) Philadelphia was the fattest city in the U.S.

2. **Just the Facts.** Check (✓) **True** or **False. If a sentence is false, change it to make it true.**

	True	False
1. John Street is overweight now.	☐	✔

John Street was overweight when he was a young man.

2. John Street was the mayor of Philadelphia. ☐ ☐

_____

3. Many restaurants in Philadelphia offer healthy food. ☐ ☐

_____

4. Mayor Street stopped exercising after he lost weight. ☐ ☐

_____

5. Many people in Philadelphia want to lose weight. ☐ ☐

_____

6. Philadelphia is the fattest city in the U.S. ☐ ☐

_____

3. **Learn New Words.** Choose the correct words. Write them on the lines.

~~became~~   continued   encourages   no longer   overweight   plenty of   program

1. John Street _____became_____ very unhappy after he read the magazine story.

2. He needed to lose weight because he was _____.

3. After he lost weight, he _____ to exercise. He didn't stop.

4. He started a _____ called Fun, Fit, and Free.

5. Fun, Fit, and Free _____ people to exercise and eat good food. The program helps people become healthy.

6. The program also teaches people to drink _____ water.

7. Philadelphia is _____ the fattest city in the U.S. John Street helped his city lose weight.

4. **Correct the Sentences.** The underlined parts of these sentences are wrong. With a partner, rewrite the sentences with the correct information.

1. John Street was the <u>fattest man in</u> Philadelphia.
   John Street was the mayor of Philadelphia.

2. When John Street was a young man, he was <u>worried about his city</u>.
   _____

3. There is information <u>in the magazine</u> about how to eat healthy food.
   _____

4. Health clubs are open in the afternoon, so people can <u>eat healthy food</u>.
   _____

5. About 30,000 people <u>live in Philadelphia</u>.
   _____

6. Some Philadelphia hospitals have free classes so people <u>can exercise</u>.
   _____

5. **Talk It Over.** Do you think Mayor Street was a good mayor? Why or why not? Write your answer on the lines and talk about it with a partner.

I think Mayor Street (was/wasn't) a good mayor because _____
_____
_____

6. **Take a Survey.** Ask your classmates this question. Count their answers and put the numbers on the chart.

QUESTION	YES	NO
Do you think Mayor Street was a good mayor?		

7. **Write It Down.** What do you like best about Fun, Fit, and Free? Why?

The best thing about Fun, Fit, and Free is _____
_____
_____

Activity Menu

1. **Tie It Together.** Look at the words below. Which words go with Chapter 11? Chapter 12? Both? With a partner, write them in the diagram below. Then add more words from the chapters.

cafeteria	~~healthy~~	~~mayor~~	restaurants
~~California~~	hospitals	online	students
exercise	junk food	overweight	teachers
fit	lunchtime	Philadelphia	worried

More words:

_____ _____ _____ _____

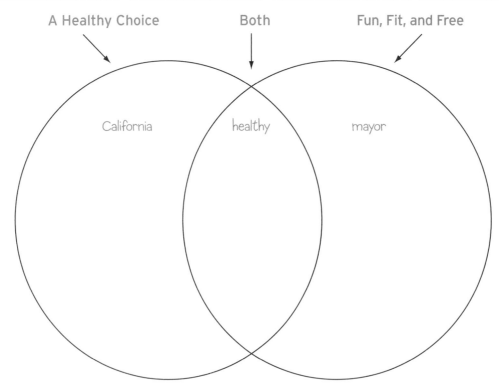

A Healthy Choice   Both   Fun, Fit, and Free

California   healthy   mayor

2. **Write It Down.** Choose three words from Activity 1 and write a sentence using each word. Underline the word in the sentence. Share your sentences with your classmates.

1. _____

2. _____

3. _____

3. **Think It Over.** Think about the stories in Chapters 11 and 12. What is the problem in each story? What is the solution? Write your answers in the chart and share them with a group.

STORY	PROBLEM	SOLUTION
A Healthy Choice		
Fun, Fit, and Free		

4. **Just for Fun.** Use the clues in the box to complete the puzzle.

2 Down spells S O L V E

Clues

Across
5. not healthy
6. where you eat at school
8. also (two words)
9. fat
Down
1. a lot
2. find the solution
3. when you eat lunch
4. tired
7. healthy

5. **Go Online.** Find a health club in your city. Use an Internet search engine like Google and type in "health club" and the name of your city. Write the name and address here:

_____

_____

CHAPTER 13

Senior Athletes

Before You Read. Look at the picture and read the title of the story.

1. **Write your answers on the lines.**

   What are these people doing? _____

   How old are these people? _____

   What is your favorite sport? _____

   Why do you like it? _____

2. **Circle your answer and write it on the line.**

   What is an athlete? _____

   a. a person who works in a restaurant

   b. a person who writes books

   c. a person who plays sports

Senior Athletes

EVERY SATURDAY MORNING, MAVIS Albin puts on her basketball shoes and goes to the gym. She **practices** for a few hours with other players. Mavis is
5 captain of her basketball team, the Tigerettes. Mavis, the oldest player on her team, is 64 years old. The Tigerettes play in the Senior Olympics for people who are over 50 years old.
10   Mavis **retired** from her job a few years ago. She wanted to be busy, but she didn't know what to do. Then one day she read a story in the newspaper about the Tigerettes, a senior basketball
15 team. She wanted to learn more about it. Mavis loved basketball when she was a student in high school. Then she got married and had a business **career** and three sons. She didn't have time to play
20 basketball anymore.

    After Mavis learned more about the Tigerettes, she practiced with them a few times. Then they asked her to **join** the team. Soon, she became the
25 captain. Mavis says, "When I started, I was **exhausted** after two minutes. Now I can run the whole game without getting tired."

    All across the country, more and
30 more seniors are playing sports. Today, people live longer. Doctors say that **exercise** is important for all people, including seniors. And they know that seniors must exercise and eat right to
35 stay healthy. Now there are 18 different sports in the Senior Olympics. These include running, swimming, and basketball. Mavis's team won three gold medals at the last Senior Olympics. And
40 Mavis is having a lot of fun.

---

1. **Main Idea.** What is the most important idea of the story? Fill in the bubble.

   Ⓐ Mavis Albin is captain of her basketball team.

   Ⓑ Mavis Albin plays basketball in the Senior Olympics.

   Ⓒ Mavis Albin retired from her job a few years ago.

2. Just the Facts. Circle Yes, No, or I don't know.

1. Some people on Mavis's team are older than Mavis.   Yes   (No)   I don't know
2. Mavis played basketball in high school.   Yes   No   I don't know
3. Mavis's husband plays basketball.   Yes   No   I don't know
4. Mavis is the captain of the basketball team.   Yes   No   I don't know
5. The Senior Olympics is only for seniors.   Yes   No   I don't know
6. Exercise is not important for seniors.   Yes   No   I don't know
7. Mavis's team practices only on Saturday mornings.   Yes   No   I don't know

3. Learn New Words. Choose the correct words. Write them on the lines.

career   exercise   exhausted   join   ~~practices~~   retired

1. On Saturday mornings, Mavis _____practices_____ for a few hours with other players.
2. Mavis got married, had a business _____ and three sons.
3. Mavis _____ from her job a few years ago. She stopped working.
4. The Tigerettes asked Mavis to _____ the team, and she became the captain.
5. When Mavis started, she was _____ after two minutes. Now she can run the whole game without getting tired.
6. Doctors say that _____ is important for all people, including seniors. Everyone should walk, run, or play a sport.

4. Finish the Sentences. With a partner, draw lines from the words on the left to the words on the right to complete the sentences.

1. Mavis practices with the Tigerettes   a. when she first started to play.
2. Mavis loved basketball   b. every Saturday morning.
3. Mavis was exhausted   c. after she retired.
4. Mavis joined the Tigerettes   d. when she had a business career.
5. Mavis did not have time for basketball   e. when she was in high school.

5. **Think It Over.** Complete the activity with a partner.

    a. Mavis read about the Tigerettes in the newspaper. She wanted to learn more about them. What do you think she wanted to know? Write three questions that Mavis asked.

      1. Who _____?

      2. When _____?

      3. Where _____?

    b. Trade your questions with another pair of students. Write answers for the other pair's questions.

      1. _____

      2. _____

      3. _____

6. **Talk It Over.** What are some activities that seniors do? Write them on the chart. Then talk about your answers with a group.

ACTIVITIES
ride bicycles

7. **Write It Down.** Pretend that Mavis Albin is your mother. Write three to four sentences about her.

Mavis Albin is my mother. She _____

_____

_____

CHAPTER 14

A New Life

Before You Read. Look at the picture and read the title of the story.

1. Write your answers on the lines.

   Where are these people? _____

   What are they doing? _____

2. What do you think about this sport? Check (✓) your answers.

WHAT I THINK ABOUT THIS SPORT			
	It's fun.		It's unusual.
	It's dangerous.		It's scary.
	It's safe.		It's exciting.

A New Life

IVONNE MOSQUERA WAS A VERY
sick child. She had cancer. Her
parents were very worried. They took
her to many doctors in Venezuela,
5 where they lived, but no one could
help her. Ivonne's parents found a new
doctor. The new doctor lived in the
U.S., so Ivonne and her parents
traveled to meet him. Ivonne was a
10 very strong girl, and the doctor knew
he could help her. The doctor
operated on Ivonne at the hospital,
and she got better.

The operation helped Ivonne, but
15 she became **blind**. However, Ivonne's
parents were very happy because
Ivonne wasn't sick anymore. She had a
new life because she was healthy
again. When Ivonne got older, she
20 decided to try many exciting things in
her new life. So, when Ivonne was a
teenager, she traveled alone to Paris
as an **exchange student**. She left her
family and school for a year and lived
25 with a French family. Ivonne wanted to
learn all about Paris. "My French family
and I learned a lot from each other.
They taught me to speak French, and I
taught them to read Braille. It was a
30 great year!" says Ivonne.

When Ivonne returned from Paris,
she did many other new things, too.
She learned to ski, dance, and play
the piano. She also decided to go
35 mountain climbing. She climbed to
the top of Mt. Kilimanjaro, the highest
mountain in Africa. Mt. Kilimanjaro is
a very difficult mountain to climb. It is
very cold on the mountain, and the air
40 near the top is very **thin**. People often
get terrible headaches. But Ivonne
reached the peak after four days.
Ivonne's life is fun and exciting, and
she is always ready to try **something**
45 new. What will she try next?

1. Main Idea. What is the most important idea of the story? Fill in the bubble.

- (A) Ivonne Mosquera always tries new and exciting things in her new life.
- (B) Ivonne Mosquera writes in Braille, plays the piano, skis, and speaks French.
- (C) Ivonne Mosquera climbed to the top of Mt. Kilimanjaro in four days.

2. Just the Facts. Circle Yes, No, or I don't know.

1. Ivonne lives in France.   Yes   (No)   I don't know
2. Ivonne speaks French.   Yes   No   I don't know
3. Ivonne can see.   Yes   No   I don't know
4. Ivonne can swim.   Yes   No   I don't know
5. Ivonne can ski.   Yes   No   I don't know
6. Ivonne went to college.   Yes   No   I don't know
7. Ivonne climbed Mt. Kilimanjaro alone.   Yes   No   I don't know
8. Ivonne reads Braille.   Yes   No   I don't know

3. Learn New Words. Choose the correct words. Write them on the lines.

blind   ~~Exchange~~   operated   reached   something   thin

1. _____Exchange_____ students go to live with different families in other countries.
2. The doctor _____ on Ivonne at the hospital because she was very sick.
3. After four days of climbing, Ivonne _____ the peak of Mt. Kilimanjaro.
4. It is very cold on the mountain, and it's difficult to breathe because the air near the top is very _____.
5. Ivonne is always ready to try _____ new and exciting.
6. Ivonne reads Braille because she is _____ and can't see.

4. Find the Answers. With a partner, use sentences in Activity 3 to answer the questions.

1. Where do exchange students live?
   Exchange students go to live with different families in other countries. _____

2. When did Ivonne reach the top of Mt. Kilimanjaro?

   _____

3. Why did Ivonne learn to dance, ski, and climb mountains?

   _____

4. Why does Ivonne read Braille?

   _____

5. Why is it difficult to climb Mt. Kilimanjaro?

   _____

6. Why did the doctor operate on Ivonne?

   _____

5. **Talk It Over.** Complete this list of the things Ivonne did. Can you do these activities? Do you want to try them? Check (✓) the correct columns. Then share your answers with your classmates.

THINGS IVONNE DID	I CAN DO THIS.	I WANT TO TRY THIS.	I DON'T WANT TO TRY THIS.
dancing			

6. **Take a Survey.** What three things in Activity 5 can your classmates do? Complete the chart.

ACTIVITIES	NUMBER OF STUDENTS
1. dancing	
2.	
3.	

7. **Write It Down.** What new activity do you want to try? Why? Write two to three sentences about something from Activity 5 or about something else.

I want to _____ because _____

_____

_____

_____

Activity Menu CHAPTERS 13 AND 14

1. **Tie It Together.** With a partner, write each word in the correct point on the star below. Then add more words from Chapters 13 and 14.

Africa	exciting	happy	operation
athlete	exercise	mountain	Paris
basketball	exhausted	mountain climbing	piano
doctors	gym	newspaper	seniors

More words:

_____   _____   _____   _____

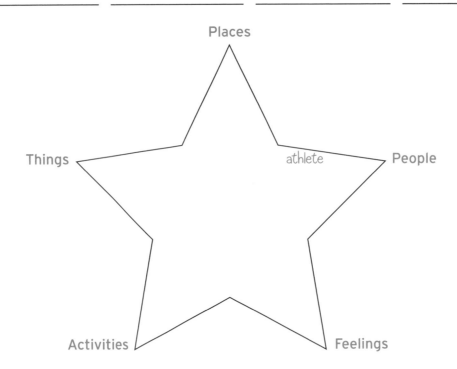

Places

Things

athlete

People

Activities

Feelings

2. **Talk It Over.** Think about the two stories. Then complete the chart below and talk about your answers with your classmates.

MAVIS ALBIN AND IVONNE MOSQUERA	
How are they similar?	How are they different?

3. **Write It Down.** Look at your answers in Activity 2. Choose one answer from each column. Then complete the sentences below.

Ivonne Mosquera and Mavis Albin are similar because _____

_____

Ivonne Mosquera and Mavis Albin are different because _____

_____

4. **Just for Fun.** Unscramble the words. Then use the numbered letters to make a new word below.

GEOLELC | C | | | | | | |
                       7   8   4

TAEM | T | | |
           5   6

SUECECD | S | | | | | | |
           2

PAKE | P | | | |
                   1   3

| B | | | | | B | | |
  1   2   3   4   5   6   7   8

5. **Go Online.** How high is Mt. Kilimanjaro? Use an Internet search engine like Google and type in "Mt. Kilimanjaro." Write your answer here.

Mt. Kilimanjaro is _____ high.

CHAPTER 15

Elephant Art

Before You Read. Look at the picture and read the title of the story.

1. **Write your answer on the line.**

   What is this elephant doing? It is _____.

2. **What do you know about elephants? Write three facts.**

ELEPHANTS
Example: They eat plants.
1.
2.
3.

Elephant Art

SENG WONG IS A YOUNG **ARTIST**. HIS **paintings** are very popular. They cost about U.S. $650.00 each. Seng Wong uses the money to take care of himself,
5 like most people. But Seng Wong is not a person. He is an elephant. Seng Wong lives in an elephant **sanctuary** in Southeast Asia. Some people try to kill elephants for their ivory tusks. The
10 sanctuary is a place where elephants can be **safe** from these people. Elephant sanctuaries are very expensive. But in Bali, India, and Thailand, the elephants help to pay for them.
15 Vitaly Komar and Alexander Melamid are famous artists. They always enjoyed unusual art. They learned that elephants often **draw** when they are **bored**. The elephants hold a stick in their trunks to
20 draw in the dirt. Renee, an African elephant in a zoo in Ohio, was their first student. Komar and Melamid taught Renee to hold a paintbrush in the tip of her trunk. She **painted** many beautiful
25 pictures, and people paid a lot of money to buy them.

When Komar and Melamid learned that elephants were in danger in Southeast Asia, they wanted to help.
30 Komar and Melamid did not have money to build sanctuaries for the elephants, so they decided to teach the elephants there to paint. They opened the Lampang Elephant Art Academy in
35 Thailand. The money from the paintings helps to pay for the Thai Elephant Center, a sanctuary near the art school. Soon, they started art schools in Bali, where Seng Wong lives, and also in
40 India. The money from the paintings helped Komar and Melamid build sanctuaries near those art schools and help many more elephants, too. Now these elephants are no longer in danger.

---

1. **Main Idea.** What is the most important idea of the story? Fill in the bubble.

- Ⓐ Seng Wong is an elephant artist that lives in a sanctuary in Bali.
- Ⓑ Komar and Melamid taught elephants to paint to pay for sanctuaries.
- Ⓒ Komar and Melamid are famous artists and they enjoy unusual art.

2. **Just the Facts.** Check (✓) **True** or **False**. If a sentence is false, change it to make it true.

	True	False
1. People buy Komar's paintings.	☐	✓

People buy Seng Wong's paintings. _____

2. Some people try to kill elephants for their paintings. ☐ ☐

_____

3. Vitaly Komar and Alexander Melamid are famous elephants. ☐ ☐

_____

4. The money from the paintings helped pay for the sanctuaries. ☐ ☐

_____

5. There are elephant art schools in Ohio. ☐ ☐

_____

6. Elephants paint in the dirt when they are bored. ☐ ☐

_____

3. **Learn New Words.** Choose the correct words. Write them on the lines.

artists   bored   draw   elephants   paint   paintings   safe   ~~sanctuary~~

1. Seng Wong lives in a _____sanctuary_____ in Southeast Asia. This is a place where elephants can be _____.

2. Vitaly Komar and Alexander Melamid are famous _____. They also teach _____ to paint.

3. Elephants often _____ pictures in the dirt with a stick. They do this when they are _____.

4. Elephants use paintbrushes to _____ at the Lampang Elephant Art Academy in Thailand. The money from the _____ helps to pay for the Thai Elephant Center.

4. Talk It Over. Talk about these questions with a partner. Write your answers on the lines.

1. Why do elephants need sanctuaries?

_____

_____

2. How did Vitaly Komar and Alexander Melamid teach Renee to paint?

_____

_____

5. Think It Over. Talk about this question with your classmates. Then write three possible answers.

WHY DO SOME PEOPLE BUY ELEPHANT ART?
1.
2.
3.

6. Write It Down. Look at the elephant's painting on the cover of this book. Do you want to buy it? Why or why not? Write two to three sentences and share them with your classmates.

I (want/don't want) to buy the elephant's painting because _____

_____

_____

_____

7. Take a Survey. Ask your classmates this question. Then count their answers and put the numbers on the chart.

QUESTION	YES	NO
Do you want to buy the elephant's painting on the cover of this book?		

CHAPTER 16

Monkey Town

Before You Read. Look at the picture and read the title of the story.

What do you know about this animal? Write three facts.

NAME OF ANIMAL: _____
1.
2.
3.

Monkey Town

ISA IS A 14-MONTH-OLD GIRL. SHE enjoys playing with her friend, Tami, several times a week. Tami is also 14 months old. Isa and Tami **share** their
5 toys and have fun together. When they are finished playing, Tami **returns** to the zoo because Tami is a baby chimp.

Tami and her family live at the
10 Monkey Town zoo near Cape Town, South Africa. Roseline Grobler, Isa's grandmother, is the owner of the zoo. Roseline **grew up** on a farm in South Africa. She always loved to play with
15 the monkeys that lived nearby in the trees. About 13 years ago, Roseline started to take care of monkeys. Some people had baby monkeys as pets because they are very **cute**. But
20 when the monkeys got bigger, they were dangerous. Then the people didn't want the monkeys anymore. So they brought them to Roseline. Roseline had so many monkeys that
25 she built the Monkey Town zoo.

At the Monkey Town zoo, there are many different kinds of monkeys. Many of the animals live in family **groups**. They are not in cages, but
30 **visitors** are. When people visit the zoo, they walk through a long cage. The monkeys are on the outside of the cage. People can stand inside the cage and **watch** the monkeys that
35 play in the trees.

Many of the monkeys here, such as the chimpanzees, are endangered. There are not many of them in the world today. This zoo keeps the
40 endangered monkeys safe, and also teaches children about monkeys. Students come from nearby schools to visit. Some of the monkeys are very gentle and friendly. The students
45 can play with these monkeys, like Isa does. Roseline hopes that one day, Isa will take care of the zoo.

---

1. **Main Idea.** **What is the most important idea of the story? Fill in the bubble.**

- (A) Isa and Tami enjoy playing together at the zoo.
- (B) Some people have monkeys as pets because they are very cute.
- (C) Roseline Grobler built the Monkey Town zoo to protect monkeys.

2. Just the Facts. Circle the correct names. Write them on the lines.

1. _____Tami_____ lives at Monkey Town.   Isa   (Tami)   Roseline
2. _____ built Monkey Town.   Isa   Tami   Roseline
3. _____ is a baby girl.   Isa   Tami   Roseline
4. _____ is Isa's grandmother.   Isa   Tami   Roseline
5. _____ is a baby chimp.   Isa   Tami   Roseline

3. Learn New Words. Choose the correct words. Write them on the lines.

cute   endangered   grew up   groups   returns   ~~share~~

1. Tami and Isa play together. They _____share_____ their toys.
2. Tami _____ to the zoo when they are finished playing. She lives there.
3. Monkeys are very _____ when they are young. That's why people like baby monkeys.
4. Roseline lived on a farm. That is where she _____.
5. Some monkeys are _____. There are not many in the world today.
6. The monkeys live together in family _____ at Monkey Town.

4. Complete the Paragraph. Use the words below to complete the paragraph.

cage   inside   outside   ~~visitors~~   watch

The monkeys are not in cages at the Monkey Town zoo, but the (1) _____visitors_____ are. When people visit the zoo, they walk through a long (2) _____. The monkeys are on the (3) _____ of the cage. People can stand (4) _____ the cage. They can (5) _____ the monkeys that play in the trees.

5. **Correct the Sentences.** The underlined parts of these sentences are wrong. With a partner, rewrite the sentences with the correct information.

1. Isa likes to play with her friend, Tami, <u>every day</u>.

Isa likes to play with her friend, Tami, several times a week.

2. Roseline grew up <u>at the Monkey Town zoo</u> in South Africa.

_____

3. Roseline always loved to play with the monkeys that lived nearby <u>at the zoo</u>.

_____

4. Some people didn't want bigger, older monkeys because they were <u>cute</u>.

_____

5. At the Monkey Town zoo, <u>the animals live</u> in cages.

_____

6. **Talk It Over.** Write three possible answers to the question below. Talk about your answers with your classmates.

WHY DID ROSELINE BUILD MONKEY TOWN ZOO?
1.
2.
3.

7. **Write It Down.** Do you like zoos? Why? Complete the sentence below.

I (like/don't like) zoos because _____

_____

_____

_____

Activity Menu CHAPTERS 15 AND 16

1. **Tie It Together.** Look at the words below. Which words go with Chapter 15? Chapter 16? Both? With a partner, write them on the diagram below. Then add more words from the chapters.

animals	danger	~~pets~~	students
~~artists~~	endangered	~~safe~~	teach
cages	farm	sanctuary	Thailand
chimps	paintings	South Africa	zoo

More words:

_____   _____   _____   _____

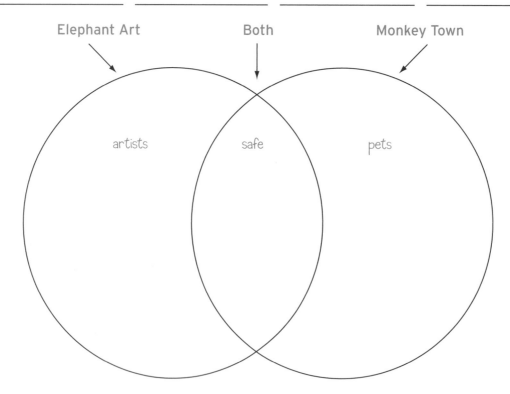

Elephant Art   Both   Monkey Town

artists   safe   pets

2. **Write It Down.** Write three sentences to show how the stories in Chapters 15 and 16 are similar. Use words from the center of the diagram in Activity 1.

1. Monkeys and elephants are safe in these stories. _____

2. _____

3. _____

4. _____

3. **Just for Fun.** Use the clues in the box to complete the puzzle.

Clues

Across

4. Elephant art schools are in Bali, Thailand and _____.
6. Komar and Melamid
8. Tami is a _____.
9. Tami lives in a _____.
10. not in danger

Down

1. ~~monkeys and elephants~~
2. a safe place
3. Roseline grew up on a _____.
5. When elephants are bored, they _____.
7. academy

4. **Talk It Over.** Some monkeys and elephants are endangered. What other animals are endangered? Make a list and talk about it with your classmates.

ENDANGERED ANIMALS		
chimpanzees		

CHAPTER 17

Take Our Daughters and Sons to Work Day

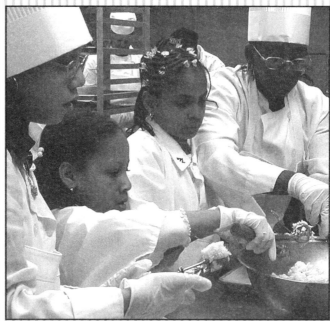

Before You Read. Look at the picture and read the title of the story.

1. Answer the questions in the chart. Write your answers on the left. After you read the story, answer the questions again. This time, write your answers on the right.

BEFORE YOU READ	QUESTIONS	AFTER YOU READ
	Who are the people in the picture?	
	What are they doing?	
	Why are the children there?	

2. Write your answer on the line.

Did you visit your parents at work when you were a child? _____

Take Our Daughters and Sons to Work Day

CARA LANG IS 13. SHE LIVES IN BOSTON, Massachusetts, in the U.S. Last Thursday, she didn't go to school. She went to work with her father instead.

5 Every year, on the fourth Thursday in April, millions of young girls go to work. This is Take Our Daughters to Work Day. The girls are between the ages of 9 and 15. They spend the day at work with an
10 adult, usually a mother, father, aunt, or uncle. They go to offices, police stations, laboratories, and other places where their parents or other family members work. Next year, the day will include sons, too.

15 The Ms. Foundation, an **organization** for women, **started** the program about ten years **ago.** In the U.S., many women work **outside** the home. The Ms. Foundation wanted girls to **find out** about many
20 different kinds of jobs. Then, when the girls grow up, they can choose a job they like.

Cara's father is a police officer. Cara says, "It was very exciting for me to go to the police station with my dad. I saw a
25 lot of people doing different jobs." Many businesses have special activities for girls on this day. Last year, Cara went to work with her aunt at the University of Massachusetts. In the engineering
30 **department,** the girls learned to build a bridge with toothpicks and candy. In the chemistry department, they learned to use a microscope. They learned about many other kinds of jobs, too.

35 Right now, Cara does not know what job she will have when she grows up. But because of Take Our Daughters to Work Day, she knows she has many choices.

---

1. **Main Idea.** **What is the most important idea of the story? Fill in the bubble.**

(A) Cara's aunt works for the University of Massachusetts.

(B) Cara does not know what job she will have when she grows up.

(C) Girls learn about different jobs on a special day each year.

2. **Just the Facts.** Circle the correct words. Write them on the lines.

1. Cara's _____father_____ is a police officer.
   aunt (father)

2. Cara's _____ works for a university.
   aunt   father

3. Right now, _____ go to work on this special day.
   only girls   boys and girls

4. Take Our Daughters to Work Day will include _____ next year, too.
   mothers   sons

5. Cara learned to build a small bridge in the _____ department.
   chemistry   engineering

6. Cara learned to use a microscope in the chemistry _____.
   department   university

7. Take Our Daughters to Work Day happens one day a _____.
   month   year

3. **Learn New Words.** Choose the correct words. Write them on the lines.

ago   find out   grow   ~~organization~~   outside   started

1. The Ms. Foundation is an _____organization_____ for women. Many women belong to it.

2. It _____ Take Our Daughters to Work Day to help young girls learn about jobs.

3. The first Take Our Daughters to Work Day was about ten years _____.

4. In the U.S., many women work _____ the home. They don't work in their houses.

5. Take Our Daughters to Work Day helps girls _____ about many different kinds of jobs.

6. Then, when the girls _____ up, they can choose a job they like.

4. **Find the Answers.** Use sentences in Activity 3 to answer the questions.

1. What is the Ms. Foundation?
   The Ms. Foundation is an organization for women. Many women belong to it.
2. What did the Ms. Foundation do?
   _____
3. When was Take Our Daughters to Work Day started?
   _____
4. What is the reason for this day?
   _____

5. **Correct the Sentences.** The underlined parts of these sentences are wrong. With a partner, rewrite the sentences with the correct information.

1. On the fourth Thursday in April, young girls go to police stations with their fathers.
   On the fourth Thursday in April, young girls go to work with adults.
2. The girls spend the day at work with an adult, usually a sister or brother.
   _____
3. Cara knows she has many choices because she goes to school every day.
   _____

6. **Think It Over.** Why do children go to work on Take Our Daughters and Sons to Work Day? Look at the reasons in the chart. Check (✓) the reasons you agree with. Then add two reasons. Share your answers with your classmates.

REASONS			
to find out about jobs		for fun	
for money			
to spend time with their parents			

7. **Write It Down.** Complete the following sentence.

I (think/don't think) that this day is a good idea for children because _____
_____

CHAPTER 18

Teamwork

Before You Read. Look at the picture and read the title of the story.

1. **Write your answer on the line.**

   What are these people doing? _____

2. **Circle your answers.**

   Teamwork means:
   a. working in an office   **b.** playing a sport   **c.** working together

   Do you think teamwork is important at work?
   a. Yes   **b.** No

   Do you think teamwork is important at school?
   a. Yes   **b.** No

   Do you think teamwork is important in sports?
   a. Yes   **b.** No

Teamwork

BEN TOY WORKS FOR A LARGE computer company. He and his coworkers are on a "scavenger **hunt**." They have a list of questions, such as
5 "What is the name of the oldest painting at the Museum of Modern Art?" They must travel around the city to find the answers. The employees **separate** into two teams. First, each
10 team **decides** where to look for the answers. For example, they can go to zoos, museums, and parks. Then they choose a person to go to each place. Everybody has a job to do so the team
15 can finish quickly. When they find an answer, they write it down. The first team that finds all the answers **wins**.

Ben and the other employees are having fun, but they are working, too. In
20 fact, Ben's boss wrote the questions for the scavenger hunt. The company is teaching the employees to work together. Many companies now have new and exciting ways to teach
25 **cooperation**, or **teamwork**. They believe that employees work better when they help each other. They can work faster and more easily, too. Companies think this is important.

30 Some companies do other fun things to teach teamwork. For example, one small company sends employees to a cooking school. The employees help each other while
35 they learn to prepare a large, delicious meal. When they are done, they sit down and enjoy the meal together. They learn to cook, and they also learn to work together.
40 Employees at another company go rock climbing. Rock climbers must work together to succeed. All the employees have a good time and learn an important lesson, too. This
45 is fun for the workers and important for the companies.

---

1. **Main Idea.** What is the most important idea of the story? Fill in the bubble.

(A) Some companies have fun ways to teach teamwork.

(B) Teamwork is important for many large companies.

(C) Ben and the other employees enjoyed the scavenger hunt.

2. **Just the Facts.** Check (✓) **True** or **False. If a sentence is false, change it to make it true.**

	True	False
1. Ben Toy is the boss of a large computer company.	☐	✓

 Ben Toy works for a large computer company.

| **2.** The employees learn to work together on the scavenger hunt. | ☐ | ☐ |

_____

| **3.** Ben's boss plans where to look for the answers. | ☐ | ☐ |

_____

| **4.** Companies teach teamwork in different ways. | ☐ | ☐ |

_____

| **5.** Some employees go to cooking schools to learn teamwork. | ☐ | ☐ |

_____

| **6.** It's important for rock climbers to work alone. | ☐ | ☐ |

_____

3. **Learn New Words.** Choose the correct words. Write them on the lines.

choose   cooperation   decides   ~~hunt~~   separate   wins

a. The company told Ben Toy and his coworkers to go on a scavenger _____hunt_____.

b. First, the employees _____ into two teams.

c. A large computer company decided to teach _____, or teamwork, to its employees.

d. Then the teams _____ a person to go to each place.

e. The first team that finds all the answers _____.

f. Each team _____ where to look for the answers.

4. **What Happened First?** With a partner, put the sentences in Activity 3 in the correct order.

a. _____   b. _____   c. __1__   d. _____   e. _____   f. _____

5. **Think It Over.** Teamwork is important for scavenger hunts, cooking, and rock climbing. What other activities are easier to do with teamwork? With a partner, write six more activities in the chart below. Share your answers.

ACTIVITIES FOR TEAMWORK	
scavenger hunts	
cooking	

6. **Talk It Over.** Separate into two teams. With your team, write a list of ten questions about your school or your class. For example, "Who speaks three languages?" or "How many computers are in the computer lab?" Then trade lists and go on a scavenger hunt.

SCAVENGER HUNT QUESTIONS	
1.	6.
2.	7.
3.	8.
4.	9.
5.	10.

7. **Write It Down.** Look at the list in Activity 5. Which activity needs teamwork most? Why?

Teamwork is most important for _____ because _____

_____

_____

_____

Activity Menu

1. **Tie It Together.** With a partner, write each word in the correct point on the star below. Then add more words from Chapters 17 and 18.

adults	cook	fun	rock climbers	uncles
aunts	enjoy	microscope	rock climbing	university
boss	exciting	museum	teach	work
bridge	~~father~~	police station	teamwork	zoo

More words:

_____   _____   _____   _____

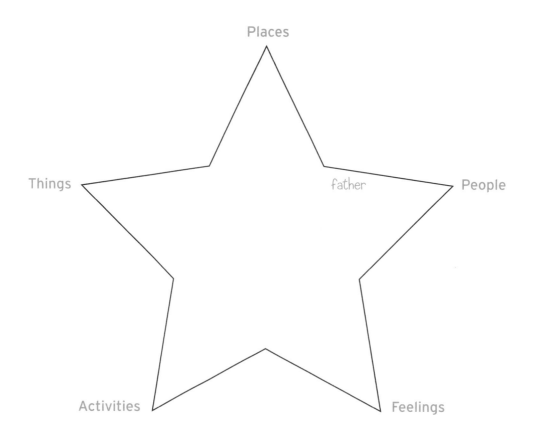

Places

Things

father   People

Activities

Feelings

2. **Talk It Over.** Talk about the stories in Chapters 17 and 18 with a group. How are they similar? How are they different? Complete the sentences.

The two stories are similar because _____

_____

The two stories are different because _____

_____

3. **Just for Fun.** Complete the activity with a partner.

a. Unscramble the following sentences.

Example:

important   It's   together   to   work   learn   to

____It's____ __important__ ___to___ ___learn___ ___to___ ___work___ __together__ .

1. fun   There   to   ways   are   teamwork   teach

_____ _____ _____ _____ _____ _____ _____ .

2. aunt   works   the   Cara's   at   Massachusetts   of   University

_____ _____ _____ _____ _____ _____ _____ _____ .

b. Now write two scrambled sentences. Ask your partner to unscramble them.

1. _____ _____ _____ _____ _____ _____

_____ _____ _____ _____ _____ _____ .

2. _____ _____ _____ _____ _____ _____

_____ _____ _____ _____ _____ _____ .

4. **Go Online.** Use an Internet search engine like Google and type in "Take Our Daughters to Work Day." What day will it be next year? Write your answer here.

_____

CHAPTER 19

The Chip Family

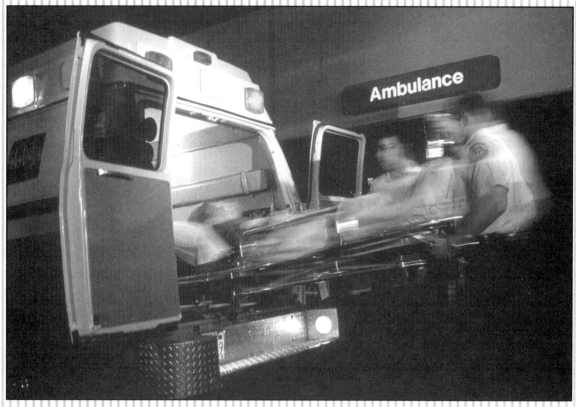

Before You Read. Look at the picture and read the title of the story.

1. **Answer the questions in the chart.**

WHO ARE THESE PEOPLE?	WHERE ARE THEY?	WHAT IS HAPPENING?

2. **Circle your answer and write it on the line.**

The person in the ambulance had an accident. The doctors in the hospital

_____ information about this person.

a. will need   **b.** will not need   **c.** will have

The Chip Family

JEFFREY JACOBS WAS VERY SICK A few years ago. After a while, Jeffrey felt better, but he **still** needed to take a lot of medicine every day. One day,
5 Jeffrey had a terrible car **accident**. An ambulance took him to the **hospital**. The doctors there needed to know some **information** about Jeffrey. For example, did he have any medical problems? Did
10 he take any medicine? Jeffrey took ten different kinds of medicine. This is important information for doctors. But Jeffrey could not speak. The doctors asked his wife, Leslie, these questions.
15 Jeffrey was lucky. His wife knew his medical information. Finally the doctors helped Jeffrey, and soon he went home.

A few years later, Jeffrey's son, Derek, saw a show on TV. He found out
20 some interesting news. Some doctors developed a small computer **chip**. The chip can hold important information about a person, such as his or her name, address, and telephone number.
25 It can also hold information about the person's medical **history**, such as the kinds of medicine a person takes. But the chip is only the size of a **grain** of rice. Doctors can put it under the skin
30 of a person's arm with a small needle. Then a computer can read the information from the chip when someone comes to the hospital.

After Derek saw that TV show, he
35 wanted computer chips for his family. He told his mother about the chip, and she agreed with him. A few months later, the Jacobs family became the first family to get the computer chips. Derek thinks that
40 the small computer chip will be helpful for his family and for other people, too.

1. **Main Idea.** **What is the most important idea of the story? Fill in the bubble.**

(A) Doctors developed a computer chip to help patients, and the Jacobs were the first to get them.

(B) Derek learned about a computer chip on TV and told his mother about it.

(C) Hospitals use computers to read computer chips when someone has an accident.

2. **Just the Facts.** Check (✓) **True** or **False**. If a sentence is false, change it to make it true.

	True	False
1. Derek Jacobs takes a lot of medicine.	☐	✔

Jeffrey Jacobs takes a lot of medicine.

2. Leslie Jacobs learned about a computer chip on TV. ☐ ☐

_____

3. The computer chips hold a lot of information. ☐ ☐

_____

4. The Jacobs will get the computer chips in a few months. ☐ ☐

_____

5. Doctors need to know a patient's medical history. ☐ ☐

_____

3. **Learn New Words.** Circle the correct words. Write them on the lines.

1. Jeffrey felt better, but he _____*still*_____ needed to take a lot of medicine.

usually (still) often

2. Doctors developed a small computer _____. It holds important information about a person.

chip   Web site   information

3. It has information about the person's medical _____, and the kinds of medicine a person takes.

school   history   accident

4. Doctors put it under the _____ of a person's arm with a small needle.

skin   hair   shirt

5. But the chip is only the size of a _____ of rice. It's very small.

grain   bowl   chip

4. Complete the Sentences. Use the pairs of words to complete the sentences.

a. problems ~~information~~

The doctors there needed to know some ____information____ about Jeffrey.

For example, did he have any medical _____?

b. speak   answer

But Jeffrey could not _____. His wife had to _____ the
questions. Finally, the doctors helped Jeffrey.

c. put   read

Doctors _____ it under the skin of a person's arm with a small needle.

Then a computer can _____ the information from the chip. Now the

Jacobs family is the first family to have the chips.

d. hospital   accident

One day, Jeffrey Jacobs had a terrible car _____. An ambulance took

him to the _____.

e. developed   found out

Jeffrey's son, Derek, _____ some interesting news. Doctors
_____ a small computer chip.

5. What Happened First? With a partner, put the sentences in Activity 4 in the correct order.

a. _____   b. _____   c. _____   d. __1__   e. _____

6. Talk It Over. Computer chips can hold a lot of information. What information do you want on your computer chip? Talk about your list with your classmates.

INFORMATION ON MY COMPUTER CHIP		
name		
address		

7. Write It Down. Complete the sentence below.

I (want/don't want) to have a computer chip in my arm because _____

_____

CHAPTER 20

The Right Time

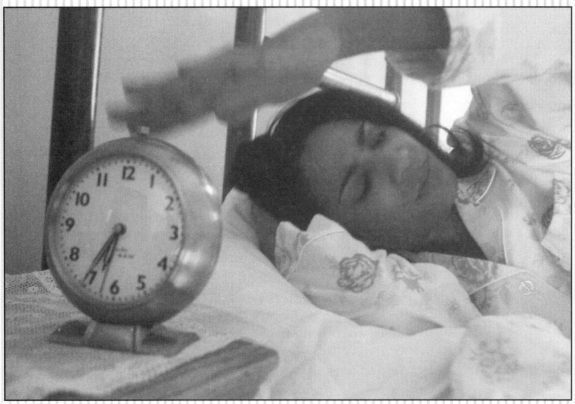

Before You Read. Look at the picture and read the title of the story.

1. **Write your answers on the lines.**

   Where is this person? _____

   What time is it in the picture? _____

2. **Answer these questions.**

QUESTIONS	WEEKDAYS	WEEKENDS
1. What time do you wake up?		
2. What time do you eat breakfast?		
3. What time do you eat lunch?		
4. What time do you eat dinner?		
5. What time do you go to sleep?		

The Right Time

MOST OF US USE ALARM CLOCKS to wake up at the right time for school or work. We look at our watches to know the right time for
5 the bus or train. However, there is also a right time to eat, sleep, exercise, and take medicine, too. We can't look at a clock for the right time for these activities. We must listen to
10 the clock inside our bodies: the biological clock.

Barbara Wells exercised every morning. She woke up at 6:00 a.m. She ran about two miles before she went to
15 work. But Barbara's legs and back started to hurt. She did some exercises before she ran. But her legs and back still hurt. She ran slower, but the pain didn't stop. Barbara talked to her
20 doctor. The doctor said, "Don't run in the morning. Try to exercise later in the day. That is the time when your body is at the right temperature for exercise. Your heart and lungs are very strong in
25 the afternoon, too." Now Barbara exercises after work. Her legs and back don't hurt anymore.

Today, doctors are learning more about chronobiology, the study of
30 biological clocks. They are learning about the **importance** of time for our bodies. For example, it is best for people to go to sleep at the same time every night and to eat only when
35 they're hungry. Also, doctors **discovered** that some illnesses, such as heart attacks, **occur** most often in the morning. This **information** tells them that the best time to take heart
40 **medication** may be at night. When patients take heart medicine at night, they may **prevent** a heart attack in the morning.

Many doctors believe
45 chronobiology can help us live healthier lives. It may be the right time to listen to these doctors!

---

1. **Main Idea.** What is the most important idea of the story? Fill in the bubble.

Ⓐ Barbara can exercise better in the afternoon.

Ⓑ It is important to listen to our biological clocks.

Ⓒ Doctors tell patients to take heart medicine at night.

2. **Just the Facts.** Complete the sentences with **in the morning, in the afternoon,** or **at night.**

1. Before she talked to her doctor, Barbara exercised ___*in the morning*___.
2. After she talked to her doctor, Barbara exercised _____.
3. Heart attacks occur most often _____.
4. Doctors tell some people to take heart medicine _____.

3. **Learn New Words.** Choose the correct words. Write them on the lines.

discovered   ~~importance~~   information   medication   occur   prevent

1. Doctors are learning about the ___*importance*___ of time for our bodies.
2. For example, they _____ new information about heart attacks.
3. They now know that heart attacks _____ most often in the morning.
4. This _____ can be very important for doctors.
5. Doctors now know that the best time to take heart_____ is at night.
6. When people take the medicine at night, they may _____ a heart attack in the morning.

4. **Correct the Sentences.** The underlined parts of these sentences are wrong. With a partner, rewrite the sentences with the correct information.

1. We must listen to the clock inside our bodies: the alarm clock.
   We must listen to the clock inside our bodies: the biological clock.
2. Your body is at the right temperature for exercise when you wake up.
   _____
3. Your legs and back are very strong in the afternoon.
   _____
4. Barbara's legs and back hurt because she ran after work.
   _____
5. It's best for people to eat three times a day.
   _____

5. **Find the Answers.** Write your answers on the lines. Share your answers with a partner.

1. Alarm clocks tell us the right time to _____.
2. Watches tell us the right time for _____.
3. Biological clocks tell us the right time to _____.

6. **Talk It Over.** Read the two statements on the chart below. Check (✓) **Agree** or **Disagree.** Then write your reasons. Talk about your answers with your classmates.

STATEMENT	AGREE	DISAGREE	REASON
1. It is best to go to sleep at the same time every night.			
2. It is best to eat only when you are hungry.			

7. **Write It Down.** Barbara Wells doesn't exercise in the morning anymore. Now she exercises after work. What change can you make in your life to feel better? How will this make you feel healthier? Write three to four sentences.

Example: I can run in the afternoon. I will feel better because my body is at the right temperature for exercise.

_____

_____

_____

_____

_____

_____

Activity Menu

1. **Tie It Together.** With a partner, use the information below to complete the chart.

INFORMATION:	
Barbara Wells	told her to exercise later in the day
~~Jeffrey Jacobs~~	didn't know his medical history
~~back pain~~	has a computer chip in his arm
see her doctor	body is at the right temperature then
couldn't answer questions	~~the hospital~~
runs after work	a car accident

THE CHIP FAMILY	THE RIGHT TIME
Jeffrey Jacobs (name)	_____ (name)
went to _the hospital_	went to _____
because he had _____.	because she had _back pain_.
The doctors _____	The doctor _____
because he _____.	because the _____.
Now he _____.	Now she _____.

2. **Talk It Over.** Barbara Wells runs every day after work. Do you think a computer chip is a good idea for her? Why or why not? Write your answer and talk about it with your classmates.

A computer chip (is/isn't) a good idea for Barbara Wells because _____

_____

_____

3. **Write It Down.** Can chronobiology be helpful to Jeffrey Jacobs? Why or why not? Complete the sentence and write your reasons.

Chronobiology (can/can't) be helpful to Jeffrey Jacobs because

_____

_____

4. **Just for Fun.** Unscramble these new words. Then use the letters in the circles to make a word in the boxes below.

CIESERXE   E □ □ □ ◯◯ □ □

TERREAPEMTU   T ◯ □ □ □ □ □ □ □ □ ◯

CCEDAITN   A □ □ ◯◯ □ ◯ □

MENBAULAC   A ◯ □ □ □ □ □ □ □

M □ D □ □ □ □ □

5. **Take a Survey.** Ask your classmates the following questions. Count their answers and put the numbers in the chart.

QUESTIONS	YES	NO
1. Do you want to have a computer chip in your arm?		
2. Do you think chronobiology can help you?		

SKILLS INDEX

READING
Chapter Topics
animals: 2, 6, 72, 76
art: 72
athletics: 32, 62, 66, 96
blindness: 66
circus: 22
dreams: 42
education: 46, 52
entertainment: 22, 26, 76
exercise: 56, 62, 96
families: 22, 26, 36, 82, 92
food: 52, 56
health: 42, 52, 56, 62, 66, 92, 96
hotels: 16
marriage: 22, 32, 36, 62
restaurants: 2, 12, 56
sleep: 42, 46
studying: 46
time: 96
twins: 12
work/jobs: 12, 22, 36, 82, 86

Comprehension
factual: 4, 8, 14, 15, 18, 24, 28, 29, 34, 35, 38, 44, 48, 49, 54, 58, 59, 64, 68, 74, 78, 79, 84, 85, 88, 94, 98, 99
inferential: 2, 6, 12, 16, 22, 25, 29, 32, 36, 42, 46, 56, 62, 82, 86, 92, 96
main idea: 3, 7, 13, 17, 23, 27, 33, 37, 43, 47, 53, 57, 63, 67, 73, 77, 83, 87, 93, 97

Critical Thinking
2, 5, 9, 10, 15, 16, 19, 20, 25, 29, 31, 32, 35, 36, 39, 41, 45, 49, 55, 59, 61, 65, 70, 75, 79, 80, 85, 89, 91, 92, 95, 99, 100, 101

Group and Partner Work
4, 5, 9, 10, 11, 15, 18, 19, 20, 21, 24, 25, 29, 30, 31, 34, 35, 39, 40, 41, 45, 49, 50, 51, 55, 59, 60, 61, 64, 65, 68, 69, 70, 75, 79, 80, 81, 85, 88, 89, 90, 91, 95, 98, 99, 100, 101

Personal Responses/Opinions
5, 9, 11, 15, 21, 25, 29, 36, 41, 42, 45, 49, 51, 55, 59, 65, 69, 75, 79, 85, 95

Pre-reading Activities
2, 6, 12, 16, 22, 26, 32, 36, 42, 46, 52, 56, 62, 66, 72, 76, 82, 86, 92, 96

Reading Through Art
2, 6, 12, 16, 22, 26, 32, 36, 42, 46, 52, 56, 62, 66, 72, 76, 82, 86, 92, 96

Reading Skills
grouping, sorting, classifying: 10, 20, 30, 40, 50, 60 70, 80, 90, 100
identifying cause and effect: 5, 9, 15, 19, 24, 29, 35, 39, 49, 50, 55, 59, 68, 75, 79, 85, 89, 95, 99, 100, 101
identifying details: 2, 4, 8, 10, 14, 18, 20, 24, 28, 34, 36, 38, 44, 45, 48, 49, 50, 54, 55, 58, 64, 68, 74, 78, 79, 82, 84, 88, 94, 98, 100
sequencing: 44, 88, 95

Taking Surveys
11, 25, 29, 45, 49, 69, 75, 101

Test-taking Skills and Strategies
fill in the blank: 15, 18, 24, 44, 48, 55, 58, 64, 68, 74, 78, 84, 88, 94, 98
fill in bubbles: 3, 7, 13, 17, 23, 27, 33, 37, 43, 47, 53, 57, 63, 67, 73, 77, 83, 87, 93, 97
matching: 35, 64
multiple choice questions: 4, 6, 8, 9, 12, 14, 16, 22, 24, 26, 28, 32, 34, 38, 39, 42, 44, 52, 54, 56, 62, 64, 68, 78, 84, 86

open-ended questions: 5, 6, 10, 15, 19, 20, 24, 25, 26, 29, 32, 36, 39, 42, 45, 50, 51, 52, 55, 65, 72, 78, 79, 80, 89, 91, 95, 98, 99
true/false questions: 4, 14, 18, 48, 54, 58, 74, 88, 94

USING THE INTERNET
Web Search Subjects
Gayle Delaney book: 51
health club: 61
Mt. Kilimanjaro: 71
roller coaster: 30
Take Our Daughters to Work Day: 91
unusual place: 21

VOCABULARY
introduction of (in story): 3, 7, 13, 17, 23, 27, 33, 37, 43, 47, 53, 57, 63, 67, 73, 77, 83, 87, 93, 97
in context (exercises): 4, 8, 14, 18, 24, 28, 34, 38, 44, 48, 54, 58, 64, 68, 74, 78, 84, 88, 94, 98

WRITING
5, 9, 10, 15, 19, 20, 25, 29, 31, 35, 39, 41, 45, 49, 51, 55, 59, 60, 65, 69, 71, 75, 79, 80, 85, 89, 95, 99, 101

PUZZLES
crosswords: 41, 61, 81
unscrambling sentences: 21, 51, 91
unscrambling words: 71, 101
word searches: 11, 31

VOCABULARY INDEX

Chapter 1
café
cage
choose
dog
favorite
popular
too
while

Chapter 2
bark
drive
exercise
get ready
take (a walk)

Chapter 3
both
confused
curly
customer
double
exactly
happened
owner
restaurant
set
special
waitress

Chapter 4
ago
guest
hotel
laboratory
regular
scuba dive
swam
underwater

Chapter 5
circus
clown
costume
dangerous
push (a button)
shoot
worried

Chapter 6
busy
(doesn't) mind
in line
roller coaster
speed
thrill
travel

Chapter 7
belong
blew off
continued
distance
marathon

Chapter 8
airline
apart
bill
doesn't matter
expensive
finish
free
most
reason

Chapter 9
carefully
dream
excited
problem
solution
strange
sure

Chapter 10
a lot
all night
at all
developing
development
forget
remember
too little

Chapter 11
cafeteria
choose
fair
gone
lunchtime
overweight
reason
solve
stopped
such as
teenager

Chapter 12
became
continued
encourage
no longer
overweight
plenty of
program

Chapter 13
career
exercise
exhausted
join
practice
retired

Chapter 14
blind
exchange student
operated
reached
something
thin

Chapter 15
artist
bored
draw
elephant
paint
painting
safe
sanctuary

Chapter 16
cage
cute
endangered
grew up
group
inside
outside
return
share
visitor
watch

Chapter 17
ago
aunt
department
engineering
father
find out
grow
organization
outside
son
started

Chapter 18
cooperation
decide
(scavenger) hunt
separate
win

Chapter 19
accident
answer
chip
developed
found out
grain
hospital
information
(medical) history
put
read
skin
speak
still

Chapter 20
afternoon
discovered
importance
information
medication
morning
night
occur
prevent